D0115769

THE RYA SAILING MANUAL

The RYA Sailing Manual

BOB BOND
National Sailing Coach
ROYAL YACHTING ASSOCIATION

PELHAM BOOKS
London

First published in Great Britain
under the title 'The Sailing Manual'
by Pelham Books Ltd
44 Bedford Square, London WC1B 3DU
June 1973
Second impression December 1973
Third impression April 1974
Fourth impression April 1976
First published in this Second Edition 1980

© 1973 and 1980 by Royal Yachting Association

All Rights Reserved. No part of this
publication may be reproduced, stored in a
retrieval system, or transmitted, in any form
or by any means electronic, mechanical,
photocopying, recording or otherwise,
without the prior permission of the
Copyright owner.

ISBN 0 7207 1131 2

Composition by Allset
Printed and bound in Great Britain by
Billing & Sons Limited
Guildford, Worcester and London

Line drawings by Dick Everitt

Contents

Preface

Revising a popular manual is always a difficult task. Since 1973 the *RYA Sailing Manual* has been the basis of all Instructor training in the UK and many other countries, and has served as the cornerstone of sound practical tuition to many thousands of experienced dinghy sailors who have given up their time to train and then teach as RYA Instructors.

The RYA Teaching Method remains virtually unaltered, but there are subtle changes of emphasis and clarification of those items which were experimental when the manual was first published.

This new edition is still a book for Instructors and those who organise sailing, but as before it will be an invaluable guide to those who are taking up sailing or who wish to improve their style.

My thanks are once again extended to those who helped me complete the original edition: Magda my wife; Gordon Fairley, General Services Manager of the RYA; Eric Twiname; Jim Saltonstall; Surgeon Commander Walters RN; Nicolas Robinson, one of our most respected Principal Race Officers; the Royal Life Saving Society; the St John Ambulance Brigade; Colin Turner of Lewmar Ltd.; Harry Cross OBE. I should particularly like to mention a new group of people: the Instructors, Senior Instructors and Coaches who have had sufficient faith in the scheme to adopt it as their own, and Sally Carmichael, my secretary, who has kept them in order.

Bob Bond
National Sailing Coach
Royal Yachting Association
May 1979

CHAPTER ONE

The Teaching Method

One of the greatest dangers is that a particular approach to the teaching of a skill can become so accepted as to become an indoctrination, or so familiar that it is taught parrot fashion without reference to its initial philosophy. The Method remains a way of introducing newcomers to sailing, the basis for training and enthusing a new Instructor, the basis for development of instructing skills.

The object of teaching people to sail is to introduce them to the sport in a way which will enable them to learn quickly and safely in an enjoyable atmosphere so that when they go away they have absorbed sufficient knowledge and have gained sufficient boat handling skills to enable them to handle a sailing boat confidently, to make simple decisions regarding weather conditions and the advisability of going afloat, to improvise in adversity and to have the enthusiasm to improve and develop new skills to become expert boat handlers. All Instructors have the unique opportunity to convert a non-sailor into a life-time enthusiast who will always remember the Instructor as the person who opened up a whole new world of opportunity and adventure.

The underlying philosophy of the Method remains unchanged – it is an ordered introduction to sailing, geared to the needs of the pupil, not the Instructor. It is arranged so that every effort of the Instructor is concentrated into getting the pupil to sail solo, and thereafter to consolidate and develop basic skills and confidence. It is designed to be taught by trained Instructors who appreciate the special requirements of pupils involving themselves in a highly technical, often seemingly hazardous sport.

Instructor Responsibility

Throughout the period that pupils are under basic instruction, the Instructor assumes total responsibility for the boat whether he is in it, alongside it, or standing on the bank. The pupil can never be held responsible for a capsize, a collision or a grounding – it is the duty of a good Instructor to ensure that the pupil sets sail with sufficient briefing as to weather, tides and hazards to operate under an umbrella of controlled safety. When instructing in the boat an Instructor should only take over the controls from a trainee when a dangerous situation threatens, and then it must be done quickly and quietly as part of a normal exercise. Once the danger passes, the trainee should be taught to cope with such a situation should it arise again.

Language of Instruction

The Method has been particularly successful in one respect – persuading the Instructor to use simple everyday words and phrases in the initial stages of instruction, relating manoeuvres afloat to those experienced ashore with other vehicles. The technical language of sailing is complicated and, being a new one to most beginners, it should be left until they are able to sail the boat. Similarly, the aerodynamic and hydrodynamic theory is complicated. An Instructor should first show that a boat can sail, then persuade the pupil to do it, then talk about the theory if there is time, or if it is relevant to do so. Obscure nautical terms confuse, and have no place in a simple approach to instructing. The boat has a 'back' and 'front' and the front moves 'towards' and 'away' from the wind when changing 'course' (a small alteration in a point of sailing) or 'direction' (a major change towards or away from the wind, as in tacking and gybing).

Advice to the pupil should be simple and consistent. The tiller is 'pulled' towards the body or 'pushed' away, the centreboard is 'pulled' down or 'pushed' up. (A daggerboard – alas – is pushed down and pulled up!) The ropes to the sail are pulled in, let out or released and fine adjustments to sails are signified by 'in a bit', 'out a bit'.

Many Instructors in training find it difficult to come to terms with having to abandon nautical language until they are faced with their first group of total beginners. An Instructor *must* be able to pass on his/her knowledge of sailing by making himself/herself understood.

Instructor/Pupil Ratio

If the pupils are paying customers, they have the right to expect value for money and if they have paid for a course of instruction which is related to a length of time they have the right to expect constant attention or supervision throughout that period.

During the initial stages of instruction afloat when pupils are learning the basic skills of steering, sail handling, points of sailing, tacking and gybing, the ideal ratio is two pupils to each instructor. As soon as pupils demonstrate their ability to sail the boat the ratio may be increased, and when only pupils are afloat and working in a group, the ratio can be increased to one Instructor in a rescue boat for each six boats afloat (one-man boats).

The RYA is often asked to draw up a table of ratios, but as so much is dependent upon individual situations, types of craft, weather conditions etc, it must be left to the Senior Instructor to make the final decision. It is his responsibility to make this decision based on the safety of the group related to the effectiveness of the tuition. Safety is dealt with in greater detail in Chapter Three – it is sufficient to state here that accidents have happened since the Scheme was first introduced, because sailing is an at-risk sport carried out in a hostile, lethal environment. The definition of an accident remains the same: an occurrence which takes place irrespective of the safety precautions taken – anything else is negligence.

Training Boats

As more RYA-affiliated sailing clubs recognise the value of teaching their new members to sail, and then to race, the range of boats used for tuition increases. The ideal training boat is one which is large enough to accommodate an Instructor and two pupils, but not so large that it is unmanageable, even when reefed, when the pupils sail solo. The majority of club boats are racing dinghies having tall rigs and large sail areas which must be reefed whilst used for training purposes, or replaced with smaller sails from a smaller boat. Handicap fleets are often willing to use their boats in the hope that the new members may decide to buy the type of boat they learned to sail in!

An interesting development in recent years has been the use of single-handed boats for group tuition, especially with boats like the 'Topper' dinghy which offer clubs and schools the opportunity of buying a group of cheap boats which can be used for basic training and race training for all ages. A number of small easily handled boats costing the same amount as one larger unwieldy boat of the same carrying capacity, will give the pupils far more enjoyment and will permit a wide range of activities. The worst thing you can do to newcomers to sailing is to put them in a boat with five other beginners so that for three-fifths of their time afloat they are virtually 'unemployed'. There is a world of difference between a wet and cold passenger and a wet and cold helmsman!

Suiting the Boat to the Conditions

Reefing has been restored to its proper place in the dinghy world. It is accepted as a normal part of seamanship and as the natural way to start off those who are learning to sail – but, just in case you happen to be a newcomer yourself, consider how you would feel about the competence of a driving instructor who asked you to step into a racing car for your first driving lesson – that's what you would be doing if asked to sail a fully rigged dinghy in medium-to-strong winds.

The essential point about reefing is that the boat can be suited to the prevailing weather conditions as well as to the capabilities of the pupils. It enables the pupils to learn in a safe environment, and as their skill levels increase the sail area can be increased proportionately. A very small area of sail can drive the boat quite satisfactorily in the early stages without destroying the 'feel' of the boat, or its handling characteristics.

The Instructor

Throughout this book the term 'Instructor' is applied to a person who trained for and has been awarded the RYA Instructor Certificate. It indicates that the holder is an experienced and competent dinghy sailor who has been trained to teach sailing afloat and ashore and understands and appreciates the special needs of the pupils under instruction. A Chief Instructor or Senior Instructor is an ex-

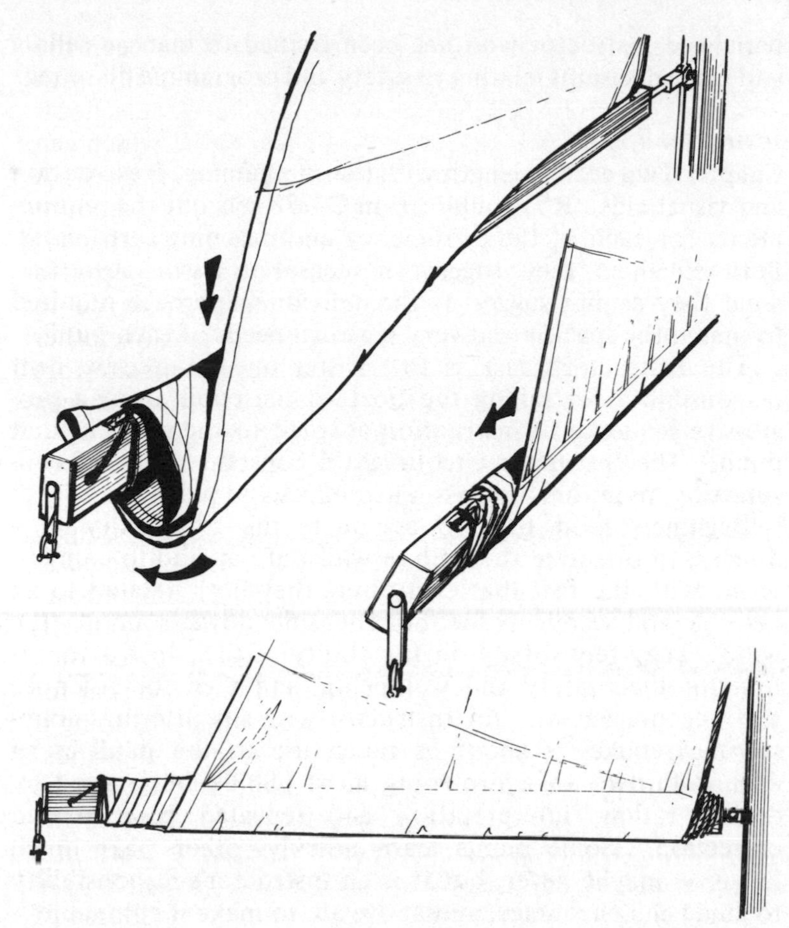

FIG. 1 Reefing to suit conditions. Taking a tuck in the sail prevents the boom sagging

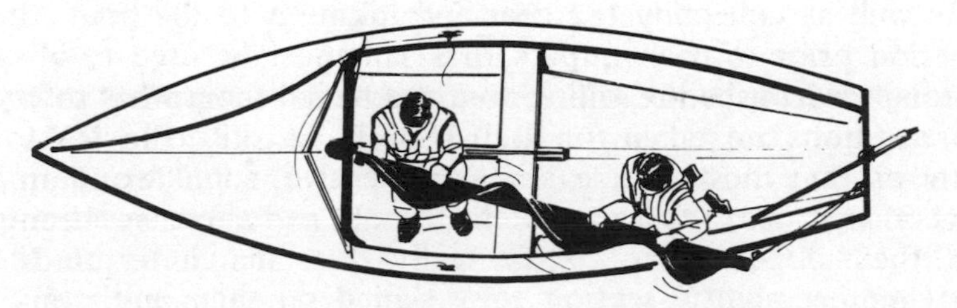

FIG. 2 Reefing afloat—this should be done in the hove-to position

perienced Instructor who has been trained to manage sailing and make decisions relating to safety and programme planning.

Instructor's Task

Chapter Two deals at length with lesson planning, presentation and visual aids. RYA publication G4/78 sets out the requirements for each of the proficiency and coaching certificates. Between them they suggest a measured lesson structure; what they cannot suggest is the individual approach required to match the specific and very personal needs of each pupil.

The Instructor's task is to transfer one-hundred-per-cent responsibility for sailing the boat to the pupil, using a progressive sequence of instruction adapted to the needs of that pupil. The Instructor encourages a constant two-way conversation, monitors progress, encourages and praises.

Beginners need time to assimilate the complexity of a dinghy, to orientate themselves whilst afloat, and to come to terms with the fact that everything they do is related to an invisible and seemingly incomprehensible power source – the wind. They rely totally on the ability of their Instructor, at first for their safety and well-being, and then for guidance and encouragement. An Instructor who sits uttering monosyllabic rebukes is about as much use to the pupil as an anchor thrown to a drowning man! Skills are learned by demonstration, interpretation and repeated practice and correction. Some pupils learn quickly, others take much longer – maybe never, but it is an Instructor's responsibility to guide and encourage, and above all, to make it enjoyable – sailing is fun!

PREPARING TO GO SAILING

As well as collecting the gear and taking it to the boat, the period prior to each pupil's first sail must be used to allay fears, to describe the sailing area and to tell them what safety precautions are taken for their benefit. A skilful Instructor knows that most people are apprehensive, some wondering whether it was such a good idea after all, and a few wondering if their dog-paddling ability really does match up to the 'swimming ability' section they signed on their application form.

It is essential that adequate and correct clothing is worn and that during the launching process the majority of pupils keep dry. Lifejackets or buoyancy aids must be worn and their fitting supervised by each Instructor for fit and suitability.

Gear Collection
Pupils collect those parts of the boat which are stored in lockers ashore. In the initial stages this allows them to handle the gear and identify it correctly, and find out where it goes and how it works. After sailing, they return the gear to its proper stowage position, having washed it and serviced it – a very important part of their training in seamanship.

Rigging
The Instructor rigs the boat on land – or on moorings – for the first outing. Questions are answered as they occur but 'knowledgeable' pupils should be reminded that they will have to restrain their undoubted talents to the pace dictated by the Instructor. Pupils assist with simple tasks – hauling the jib, attaching shackles and sliding the sails on to the spars. Everything is done from outside the boat and as the main purpose is to get afloat quickly the Instructors set the pace and do most of the work, talking as they go.

Rigging afloat requires a greater degree of organisation, including launching and sometimes rowing and anchoring – try to avoid it on the first sail. If the boat is kept on moorings give each pupil a simple task.

Launching and Recovery
Launching is always a difficult task even for an experienced crew; more damage is done to boats at this stage than at any other time. Whilst the Instructor is in charge for the first few sails, the pupil must be shown how to do things in sequence – from placing the boat on its launching trolley and how and why the bow must be secured, right through the launching and recovery sequence until the boat is stowed away with its cover in place. It must be demonstrated and practised until a routine is established. Particular emphasis should be placed on the need to keep launching sites free of

empty launching trolleys and the common sense of establishing a traffic flow if a large number of boats are sharing the same launching facility. In normal circumstances the crew will hold the bow of the boat once it is afloat so that it is head to wind, and the Instructor will hoist the sails and prepare the boat for sailing.

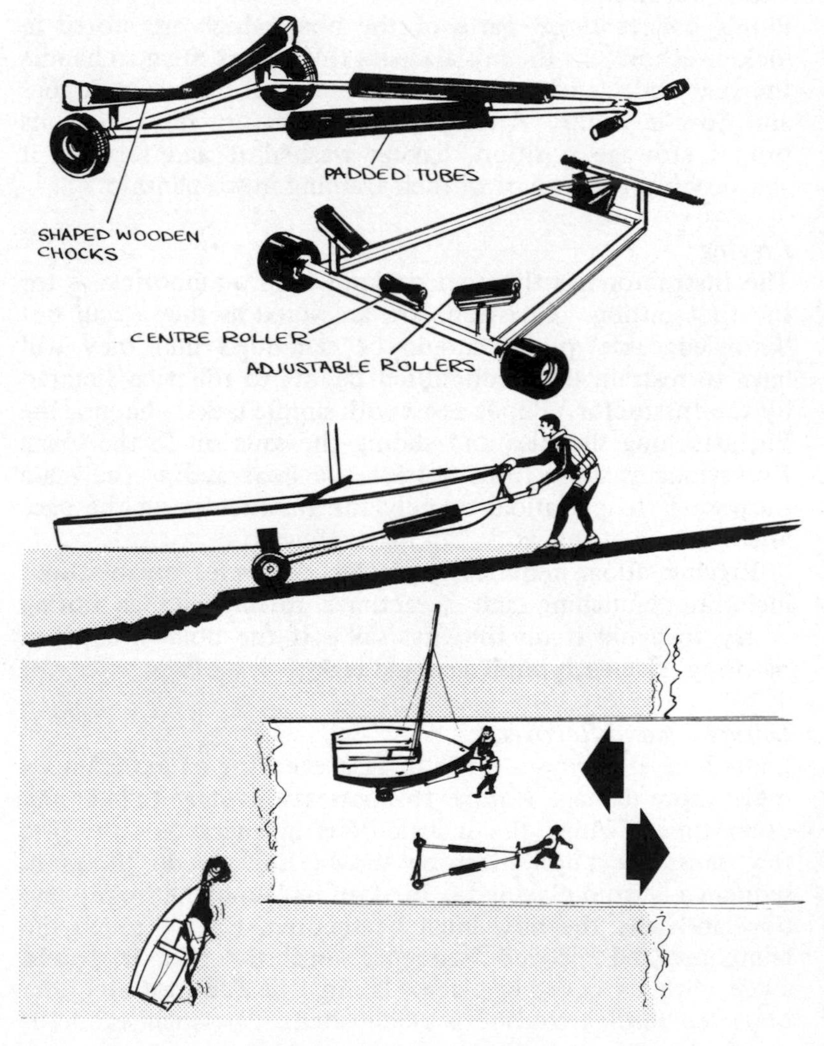

FIG. 3 Launching the boat

Lee and Weather Shores
Though not strictly part of a teaching method lee and weather shores play such a large part in launching and recovery operations that they need more than just a mention. If, for instance, the first day of a sailing course experiences strong onshore winds, the Instructor will be faced with a situation which may require the boats to be anchored off prior to the pupil going afloat, or for the pupils or Instructor to row them out, or maybe for the Instructor to sail the boat away.

FIG. 4 Lee and weather shores

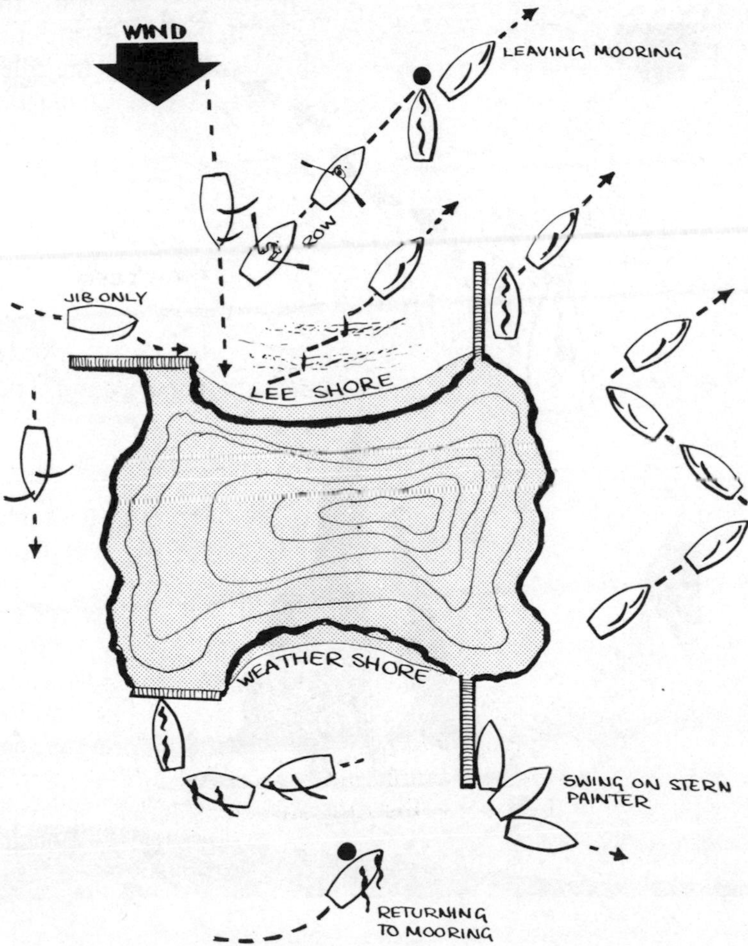

Obviously anything more than a brief reference to alternatives would be beyond the understanding of most of the pupils, so whichever course of action is decided upon by the Chief Instructor it should be explained to the pupils and then carried out. Later in the course, lee and weather shores will be dealt with in detail by the Instructor, but where pupils are liable to get very wet, as in getting away from a lee shore on a gently sloping beach, the Instructor should warn the pupils prior to launching.

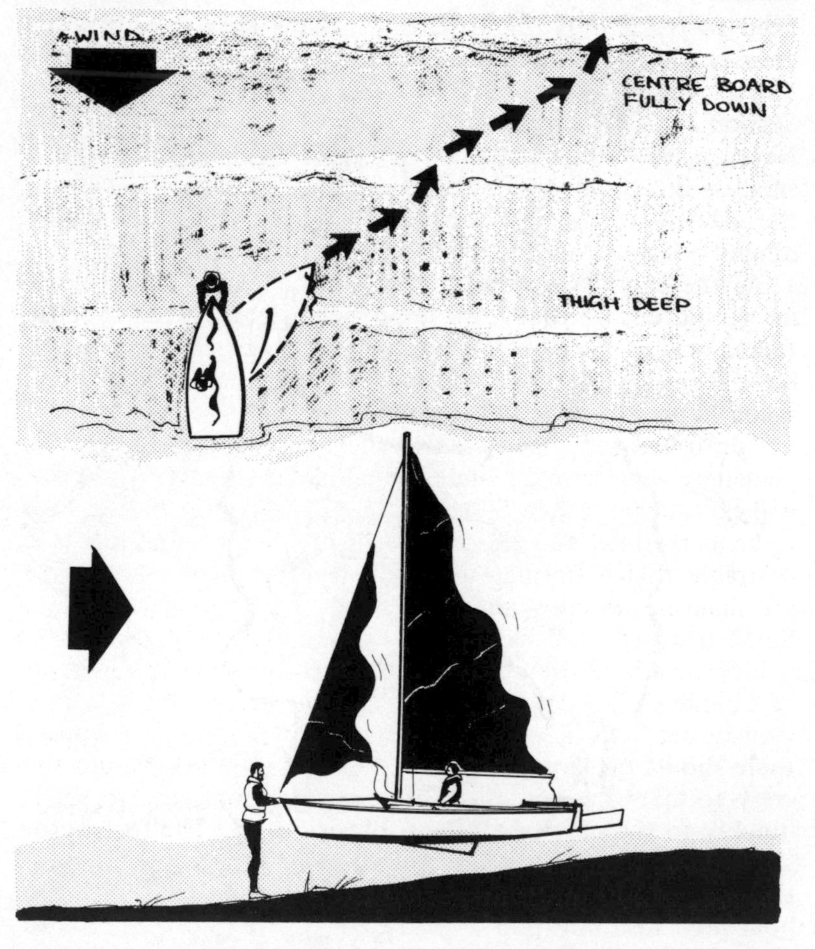

FIG. 5 Getting away from a lee shore

SAILING SESSIONS

Whenever pupils go afloat or have a shore session they should revise previous work and should be taught something new. The sessions have been arranged to ensure that they have every opportunity to demonstrate their ability and to learn at least one new sailing skill. Pupils dictate their own pace of learning. Many Instructors make the mistake of trying to teach too much in a week, or work on the theory that once they have demonstrated a particular skill, pupils will automatically repeat it. Experienced Instructors recognise the need to teach only the essentials. Experience or additional courses will consolidate the basic skills.

Session 1 – Familiarisation

Never assume that pupils have previously been afloat in a small sailing dinghy. The difference between stepping on to the side of a passenger ferry and the side of a small sailing dinghy is a wet shirt and a broken nose!

As the Instructor will be sailing the boat for this session, he should ensure that both crew members are given specific tasks, one as crew, the other as passenger. The crew will be responsible for controlling the jib and centreboard when asked to do so by the Instructor.

Controlled movement inside the boat is important. The passenger will normally slide along the centre seat. The crew will be taught to face forwards or aft, depending on the task to be performed and the type of boat. As a general rule it is desirable that helmsman and crew face the same way. With aft mainsheets, crew and helmsman face aft when tacking. Some Instructors dislike this, because, for a moment no one is looking where the craft is going. However, in the process of tacking, the boat is turning into the area which has previously been checked by both crew and helmsman, therefore there should be very little risk. Tacking facing aft enables the crew to take the new jib-sheet across the boat, and to set it quickly to the new tack when told to do so. The Instructor should demonstrate the movement within the boat and ensure that crew and passenger practise. This can be done with the boat next to a pontoon or in the basic hove-to position. The aim of the session is to take the pupils out for a short sail so that they can get the feel of a sailing dinghy. It should last ten to fifteen minutes. During this time the Instructor talks about things outside the boat and changes direction three or four times. Crew and passenger change roles halfway through the session.

Terminology. During this lesson the Instructor will refer to: the seat, small sail, the ropes to the small sail, which should be 'pulled in', 'let out' and 'released'; and the centreboard, which will be pushed up and pulled down, and the front and back of the boat.

Teaching Points. This session introduces the pupil to the boat. Ensure that it is incident free and *short*! Pupils are often thankful to get their feet back on firm ground. Never under-estimate the value of a joy ride. It is a pleasure to be sailed around by a competent, informed Instructor.

It is very important that the whole group is taken out for the joy ride in crews of two, in rapid succession.

Session 2 – Orientation

The Instructor sails the boat to the designated sailing area, revising crew movements during changes of direction. When the boat arrives at the sailing area it is brought to a stop on a course slightly to windward of a beam reach by letting the sails out until they flap. For convenience we call this position a *basic hove-to position* (Fig. 7). It is invaluable to Instructors and pupils alike, giving a known reference point from which the boat can be sailed away easily. The Instructor points out prominent sea and land marks which should be referred to constantly throughout this and subsequent sessions. Correct orientation at this stage is vital. It is especially important to locate the sailing base or point of departure. A launching point may seem an obvious feature when launching the boat but, from the water, it is a small part of the landscape.

Basic Point of Sailing. All initial teaching is carried out on a beam reach, thus enabling a very shallow figure-of-eight course to be set. Going about (changing direction into the wind) from a reach to a reach ensures that the pupil must learn to steer the boat throughout the manoeuvre. Because the boat turns through an arc of 180° (Fig. 6) it gives the pupil time to move across the boat and allows sufficient time to correct mistakes. If the pupil fails to carry out the manoeuvre correctly the boat will stop head-to-wind.

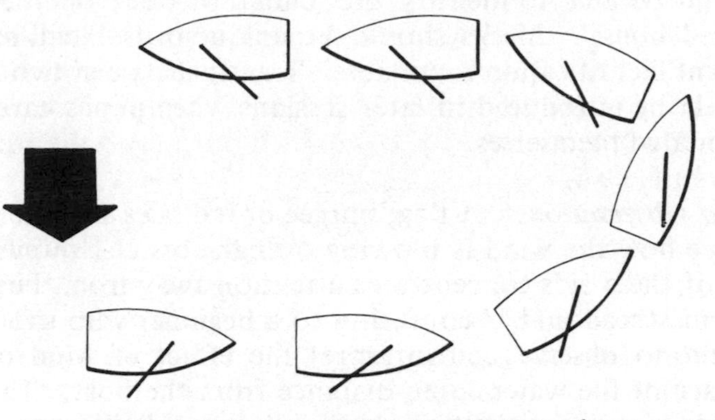

FIG. 6 Going about, from reach to reach

Teaching Points. In the basic hove-to position the boat is at 80° to the wind so that the fully eased mainsail weathercocks (Fig. 7). This is a safe position from which it is easy to obtain immediate control. It is used whenever instructions are given to pupils or to facilitate demonstrations of particular manoeuvres. It is very valuable to the pupils during and after

FIG. 7 Basic hove-to position

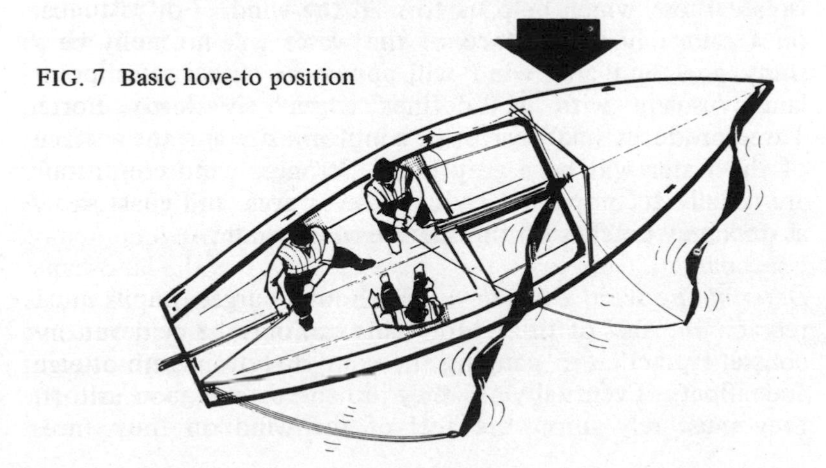

their solo sail, enabling them to recover from their mistakes. They should be taught to regard it as a refuge. Fully explained by a competent Instructor, it is a position which allows them, in emergency, to gather their often scattered wits!

Sea and land marks should be chosen carefully. Pupils should be able to identify the 'clump of trees' or 'the blue-gabled house'. Marks should be unique or isolated, so that instant identification is possible. Transits between two marks should be introduced in later sessions when pupils have fully orientated themselves.

Wind Observation. A flag, burgee or tell-tales are often used to see how the wind is blowing over the boat. However, the use of these aids concentrates attention away from the sea to the masthead and is confusing to a beginner who should be taught to observe and interpret the effect of wind on the surface of the water some distance from the boat. This will enable him to anticipate violent gusts or a lull. Wind patterns are not easily identified on the surface of the water, because there are so many other things which must be taken into consideration. However, it is vital that, during all the initial teaching, the Instructor assists the pupil in correct identification of wind patterns. A stronger gust normally shows as darker moving patches, often called 'cats'-paws' because of the way they fan out. A lull will show up as a lighter 'oily patch'. As most waves are wind-made, it is important to isolate those which help us to read the wind. For instance, on a calm day the surface of the water will normally be a shiny grey and any wind will appear as darker patches or lanes, usually with well-defined edges. A steady Force Three produces small waves of a uniform size and the surface of the water will be a grey blue. Stronger wind conditions are usually accompanied by confused waves, and gusts show as dark grey patches on the surface of the water.

Determining Wind Direction. Without a burgee, pupils must rely on the feel of the wind. This can only be achieved by constant practice in gauging the wind direction both ashore and afloat. Eventually, if they are to become good sailors, they must rely upon the feel of the wind on their face.

Initially, pupils may be helped by a wetted finger, which feels cold on the side nearest the wind, or by observing flapping sails, or the surface of the water. *A pupil, who does not know where the wind is, cannot hope to sail a boat correctly.*

Session 3 – Basic Boat Control

The boat is sailed to the sailing area, Sessions 1 and 2 being revised *en route*. The aim of this session is to demonstrate the effects of the sails, rudder and centreboard. All movements of the boat are related to the wind, either turning towards it, or away from it.

From the basic hove-to position, the crew 'pulls in' his sail so that the boat moves forward and the front of the boat moves away from the wind. The crew 'lets out' his sail, the Instructor pulls in the large sail, the boat moves forward. The front of the boat moves towards the wind, crew and passenger change places and repeat a number of times. From the basic hove-to position, the boat is sailed on a beam reach. The Instructor demonstrates the effect of moving the tiller away from him, which causes the front of the boat to move towards the wind. When he pulls the tiller towards him, the front of the boat will move away from the wind.

He also demonstrates what happens when the tiller is centred at any stage during the turn. The Instructor steers a wavy path and centres on different positions on new courses.

Crew Practice. When it is time for the crew to change positions, the person about to take control moves along the outside of the boat, thus enabling him to take control quickly in the event of an 'epic' (Fig 8). Pupils alternate as helmsman,

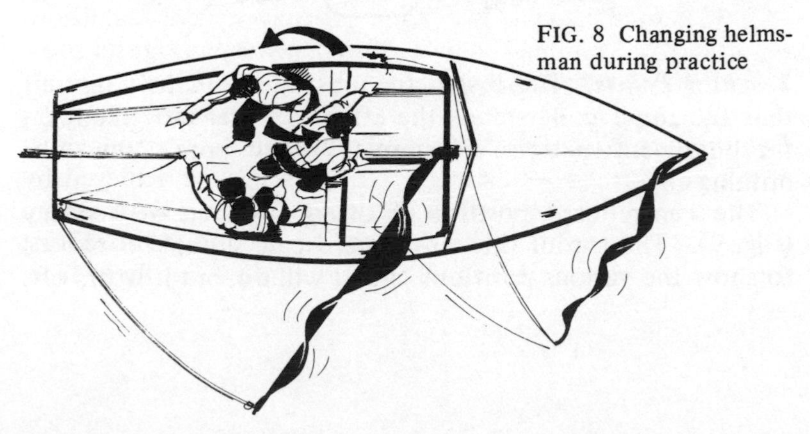

FIG. 8 Changing helmsman during practice

each practises the manoeuvre, with sails and tiller, to get the feel of the main controls.

Centreboard Control. During the initial period the centreboard is in the fully down position whilst manoeuvres are carried out. However, since it has such an important part to play in boat handling, its effect must be demonstrated to the pupils. Sailing on a beam reach, left, largely, to itself, the boat changes direction into the wind. The Instructor points out how the boat steers a circular course, on to the opposite beam reach. The centreboard is raised by the crew and the manoeuvre is repeated. It will be found, of course, that the boat will have great difficulty in going about, because it slides over the surface of the water. Some boats may succeed in going about but, when they do so, they are blown sideways until sufficient speed is gained to take them on a reciprocal beam reach. It is essential that this particular manoeuvre is included in each revision session, since the majority of beginners usually have difficulty in recognising no-centreboard situations.

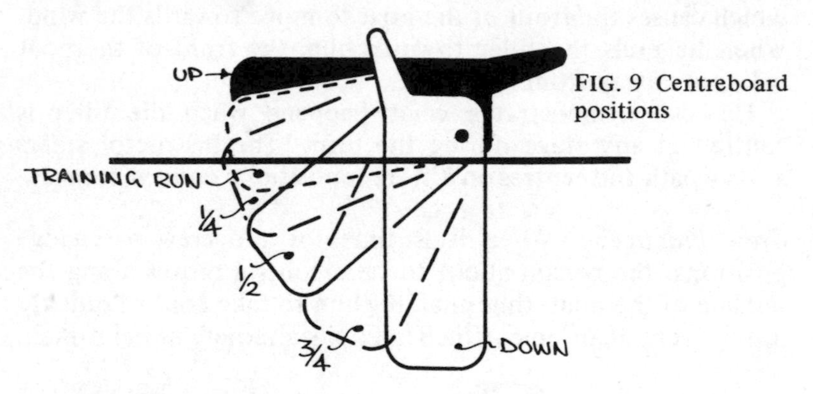

FIG. 9 Centreboard positions

Teaching Points. The Instructor must always satisfy himself that the pupil understands the effect of tiller movement on the boat. Instructions are simple: 'Away from', 'towards'; nothing else.

The centreboard position is often a source of mystery (Fig. 9). The top of the centreboard case should be marked to show the various positions. Paint will do, but it wears off.

It is often better to scribe the case and fill it with a contrasting paint or filler. It is not necessary to propound the *theory* of the centreboard until later sessions.

The 'No-Go' Zone. Following the no-centreboard demonstration, during which the boat succeeded in stopping head-to-wind, the Instructor continues the theme by demonstrating that the boat will sail with the wind, across the wind but not against the wind. The boat is brought into a close-hauled position, sails set correctly. A wavy course is steered (Fig. 10) so that the boat is constantly crossing the boundary of the 'No-go' zone and passes from a sailing to a non-sailing position. Great emphasis must be placed on the movement of the tiller particularly noting that, to bring the boat into a sailing position, the tiller must be brought towards the helmsman's body. The French liken the limits of the 'No-go' zone to the corner of a glass-fronted shop.

It helps to define the limits of the 'No-go' zone by dropping a marker buoy or using a mooring. Sail away from it on opposite close-hauled tacks, pointing out land marks on both headings and for the wind direction. This helps to define the zone in practical terms afloat and to point it out on a chart or diagram ashore.

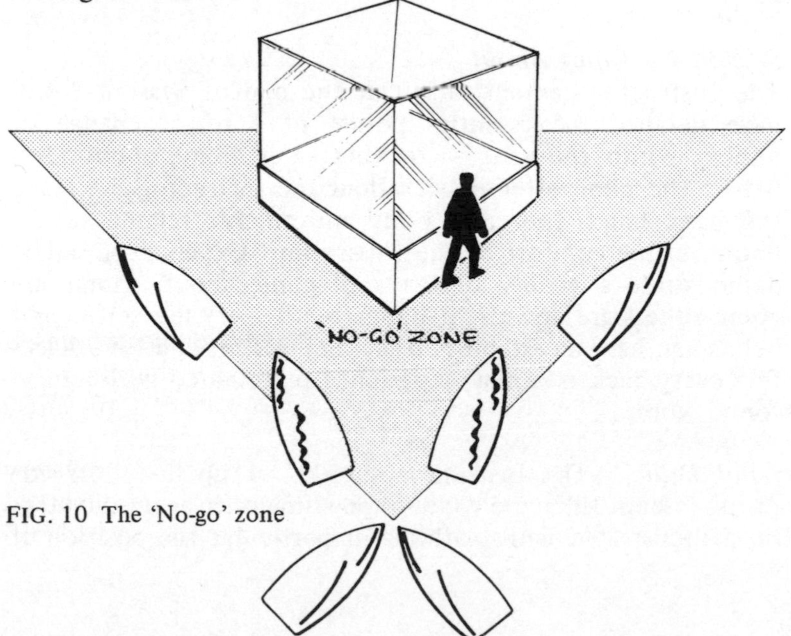

FIG. 10 The 'No-go' zone

First Phase of Learning to Sail. It is as well to consider what we have now done to our beginners. They have been introduced to the sport with the minimum amount of fuss and confusion. Instructors have avoided the complicated language of sailing, possibly to the disappointment of those who came to learn sailing as a social grace (their day will come when they are sailors). Safety and care of the boat have been given their rightful top priority. When afloat our beginners have been given time to gather their wits and have been put to work, learning first to recognise the tools of their trade and then how to use them. The basic facts of wind direction are established, and thereafter all boat movements are related to it. Everything they do is designed to be a first but essential step. The basic hove-to position is a convenient stopping point for the Instructor but may become a vital safety factor for the novice in a moment of crisis.

Pupils have participated in the action. This is *essential* if their interest is to be retained. They are already becoming aware of the need to look outside the boat for signs which will help them to anticipate correct movement and manoeuvres. They are learning to relate themselves to their environment. The final session provides a demonstration of going about.

Session 4 – Going About

The Instructor demonstration at the end of Session 3 will have detailed the essential points of a major change of direction into the wind – tacking – or 'going about', but before the pupil attempts it afloat the Instructor can teach the basic hand, foot and body movements related to the boom, in the comfort of the classroom. Experienced sailors demonstrate a variety of ways of going about. Some are good, others are downright dangerous – very few self-taught helmsmen have an established tacking routine and for a select few every tack is a new experience punctuated with a new-found word.

Land Drill. The Instructor should set up the shore-side props – seats, tiller and rope – and show once again the tacks he demonstrated whilst afloat, in particular the position of the boom at the reference point for each part of the sequence.

Experience has shown that the first few demonstrations should be done at normal speed with no explanation otherwise pupils tend to adopt the very extended sequence used by Instructors when they are demonstrating each step. The final scene-setter prior to pupil participation is a summary of the various tasks involved when going about.

The boat must be steered throughout the turn onto its new course, the helmsman and crew must move from one side over to the other, balancing the boat as the wind pressure is lost, and then regained on the opposite side of the sail. The helmsman must change tiller and mainsheet to opposite hands in such a way that, when he sits down, he will have immediate control of the boat. The crew must release the old jib sheet, pick up and adjust the new one, the centreboard may need to be adjusted. During all this activity, both have to keep a constant look out for other boats and dangers. Without doubt 'going about' is the key to sailing, therefore great care has been taken to devise a method which is simple yet effective.

The land drill permits controlled demonstration and practice. The pupil learns the skill correctly and does not move to the next stage until he can demonstrate this skill. Instructors can move easily from group to group, correcting and demonstrating, encouraging and explaining. Everyone can get individual attention.

Of course, Instructors will have evolved their own gear for land drill but it can be as simple as two chairs, a broom handle for the tiller and some electric flex, or old rope, for the mainsheet. The important thing is that the land drill can be demonstrated anywhere, utilising whatever is at hand. Some Instructors have made up permanent teaching aids from rear portions of old boats or special simulators. For our purposes we have to use another pupil as the tiller pivot! The props are arranged (Fig. 11), and adjusted as required. The land drill is designed to teach the basic principle with aft mainsheets. Modifications will be discussed later to suit particular requirements, wider boats, tiller extensions, centre mainsheets.

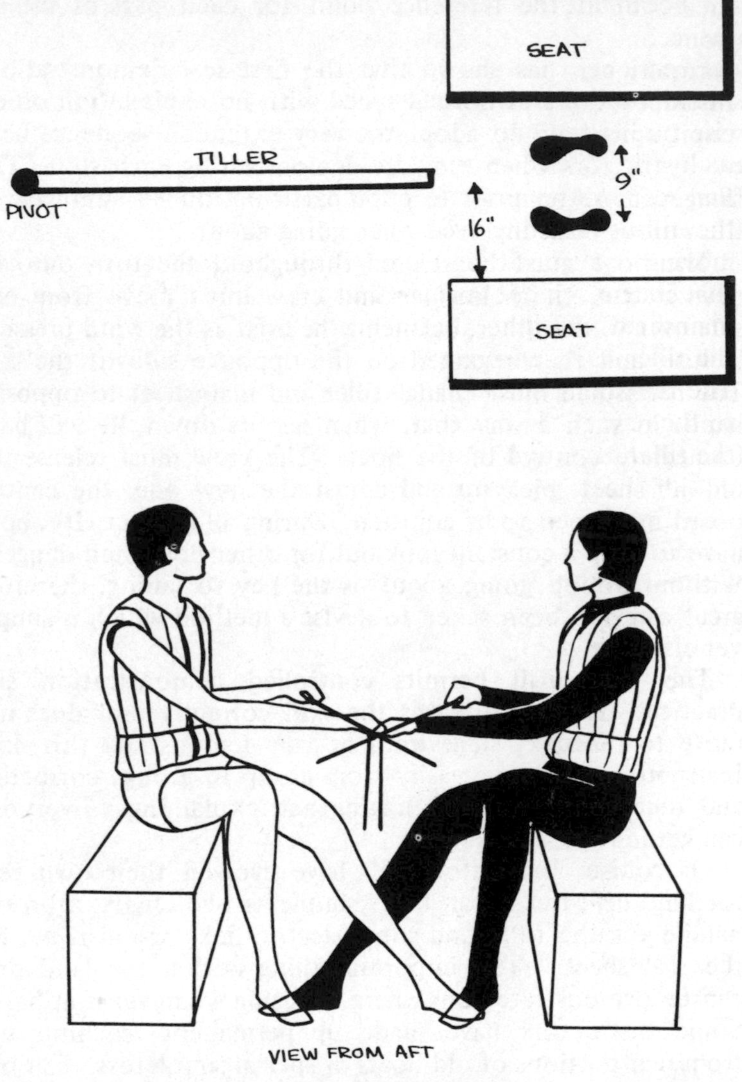

FIG. 11 Land drill 'props'

Stage 1. The helmsman faces the tiller, placing his feet in the position shown. Pivoting on his feet he sits first on one chair, then on the other. When in the seated position the back leg nearest the tiller is bent at the knee, seemingly tucked under the seat. The front leg is extended. Movement from one chair to the other will soon demonstrate how naturally this position is attained. When demonstrating, the Instructor stresses the phrase 'front foot forward' so that the pupil is in no doubt where this foot should be.

Stage 2. From the seated position, the helmsman grasps the tiller with the hand nearest it (Fig. 12) and practises moving it towards, and away from, his body, thus ensuring that its movement is not restricted. He then picks up the mainsheet with his other hand, and leads it over the back of the tiller hand ensuring that the rope is two inches above it. The remaining spare mainsheet is allowed to fall into the area to the rear of the back foot, being fed down the hole between the tiller hand and the pupil's side.

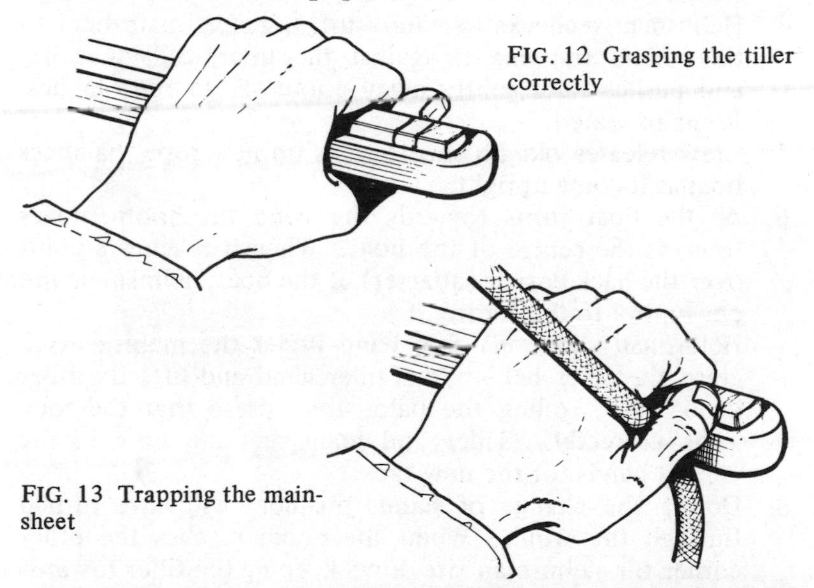

FIG. 12 Grasping the tiller correctly

FIG. 13 Trapping the mainsheet

The mainsheet is adjusted by lowering it to the back of the tiller hand and trapping it on the top of the tiller with the thumb of the tiller hand (Fig. 13). The mainsheet hand is then used to pull in, or let out, additional mainsheet.

Stage 3. Changing direction into the wind is called 'going about' or 'tacking'. The important concept is that the boat moves under the sails, which remain flapping throughout the manoeuvre.

Before each change of direction the following checks are made: that the controls are in the correct hands; that the feet are in the correct position; and that the body is facing across the boat.

It is not intended that the manoeuvre should be taught or carried out by numbers, but for clarity it has been set out in a numbered sequence.

1. Helmsman checks inside and around the boat to ensure that it is safe to tack.
2. When it is safe to tack helmsman calls 'Ready about'.
3. Crew checks all around the boat especially to windward, replies 'Yes', and uncleats jib sheet.
4. Helmsman rechecks to windward, transfers mainsheet to tiller hand trapping it against the tiller, calls 'Lee ho' and pushes tiller gently away about six to nine inches. Remains seated.
5. Crew releases old jib sheet, picks up new rope, balances boat as it come upright.
6. As the boat turns towards the wind the boom moves towards the centre of the boat. When it reaches a point over the back corner (quarter) of the boat, helmsman and crew move to the centre.
7. Helmsman slides his free hand under the mainsheet to grasp the tiller behind the tiller hand and lifts the tiller hand away, rolling the palm upwards so that the rope leads correctly. Tiller and mainsheet are now in the correct hands for the new tack.
8. During the change of hands the boat will have turned through the wind. When the boom reaches the other corner the helmsman sits down keeping the tiller towards the body until the sails fill on the new course. Helmsman centres the tiller and checks the horizon.
9. Meanwhile the crew balances the boat and pulls the jib sheets when told to do so by the helmsman, or when the boat is obviously sailing its new course.

Teaching Points. The demonstration must be correct, the

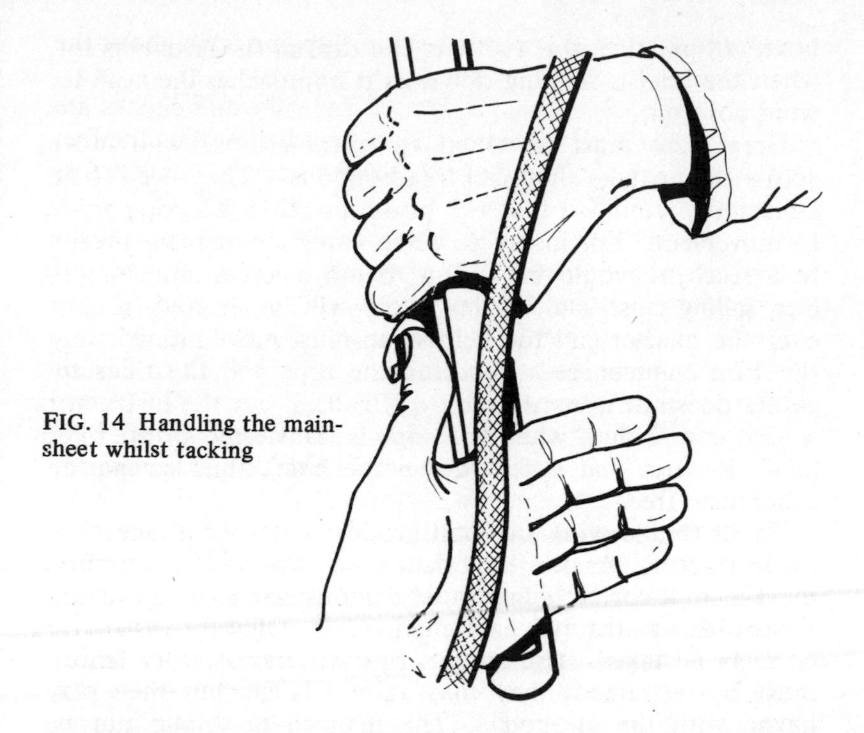

FIG. 14 Handling the mainsheet whilst tacking

'talk-through' concise and to the point. Great care must be taken by Instructors to ensure that the simple talk-through is not embroidered upon. The manoeuvre must be demonstrated a number of times to emphasise different points. One of the demonstrations must repeat the fluid movement of the manoeuvre which, for training purposes, has been broken down into a number of separate related movements.

It is important that the relationship between boom position and movements of the helmsman is established early in the teaching. The sweep of the free hand, as it is placed on the tiller, must be exaggerated. The wrist-lock position which follows, and the resulting stability of the helmsman in the boat, must be emphasised.

Most beginners have a tendency to centre the tiller whilst moving across the boat. It should be kept in its original 'away' position or, better still, should be moved a little further away as the helmsman stands up to move to the centre of the boat. In practice, this tightens the turn at the critical point, when the boat is slowing down as it approaches the head-to-wind position.

Great care must be taken to restrain those who move across the boat, as they call 'ready about'. They need to be constantly reminded that the boom position is a good guide to movement. For instance, when going about from a reach to a reach, it would be wrong to move across immediately but, sailing close-hauled, the boom will be sheeted in tight over the quarter and the helmsman must move immediately the turn commences. Handling the rope and the tiller together does not present many difficulties, but the Instructor should ensure that, when the rope is transferred to the tiller hand, the free end is fed 'down the hole', thus leaving the other hand free.

Pupils should work in small groups, under the direction of an Instructor. As the land drill is so important, each pupil must learn it correctly and must demonstrate to the group by talking his way through each manoeuvre. Only the Instructor corrects mistakes. (Budding script writers, or story tellers, must be restrained; they may raise a laugh, but they play havoc with the Method). The manoeuvre should not be attempted afloat until each pupil really understands the reasons for the movements.

Session 5 – Practice Afloat

Before going afloat, the Instructor runs through the land drill again. As the boat is being sailed to the sailing area, previous sessions are revised.

The Instructor demonstrates going about, answering any questions which may arise. The boat is placed in the basic hove-to position, the crew becomes the helmsman, passenger moves to crew position. Instructor moves to instruction position to leeward. The pupils take turns to practise, the Instructor corrects where necessary.

Teaching Points. When the pupils go afloat, it is important that their first attempts at 'going about' are successful. They will be concentrating on the mechanics and, therefore, special emphasis must be placed on the need to keep a careful look-out. The crew will require guidance in his movements. It is a simple matter to slide him along the seat until he gets it right. The helmsman must be kept working in a relatively confined sailing area. There is no merit in going about once in every ten minutes. The aim is to practise until perfect.

Session 6 – Co-ordination of Movement
This session may take up many lessons afloat. The aim is to teach the pupils to co-ordinate their movements into a smooth-flowing manoeuvre related to the wind. It should be practised until it is correct. Instructors have found that it oftens pays to bring the pupils ashore after a short lesson afloat. In this way, it is possible to repeat the land drill, and pupils then find that it means much more to them. The subsequent session afloat often reveals a considerable improvement in performance.

Session 7 – Giving a Purpose to 'Going About'
A point will be reached when the Instructor judges that the pupils are ready to move on to the next stage. This is an extremely important decision. It marks the point where we turn from teaching mechanical skills to tactical skills. Care must be taken to select a sailing area which has a mark to windward. On the open sea it may be necessary to lay a special mark. In other cases prominent land marks should be used.

Up to this point, pupils have been practising going about from a reach to a reach. The next task is to work them from a reach to close-hauled, in two or three definite changes:

1. tack from a reach to a reach;
2. bring boat to a close reach;
3. tack close reach to close reach, three times;
4. bring boat to a fetch (just off a close-hauled course);
5. tack fetch to a fetch, three times;
6. bring boat to close-hauled;
7. tack close-hauled to close-hauled, five times.

Crew changes with helmsman, the manoeuvre is repeated. It is important that each helmsman relates the new headings to land marks and that sufficient sea room is allocated to complete the sequence. If, during the manoeuvre, the boat reaches a windward shore, the Instructor sails it back to the starting point talking about the previous work. (This is standard procedure until pupils are taught downwind sailing.) When the starting point is regained, the pupils are then asked to sail to a windward land mark. Instructors should allow every opportunity for the pupils to attain the windward objective without paying too much attention to the set of the sails or the course sailed. Let the least-able pupil attempt to sail to a windward objective first, success will mean much more to him than to a pupil who has already worked it out. When both pupils have practised this manoeuvre, a period of concentrated instruction should follow, until *both* have grasped the essentials of working the boat against the wind. It often helps to sail on a fetch at this point. Thus allowing for wind shifts which would otherwise confound a close-hauled beginner, deprived of his wind.

Teaching Points. At this stage the following names should have been introduced: mainsail, mainsheet, jib, jibsheet, windward, leeward, shrouds, forestay. The only theory that should be taught at this stage is the simple fact that, to sail properly, the sails must be kept at a constant angle to the wind (Fig. 15). Complicated theory confounds. It is better to regard the sail as a deflector plate which provides forward drive. Sideways drift is combated by the centreboard. Instructors should accept that correct sail trim is not essential at this point, but sufficient drive should be obtained from the

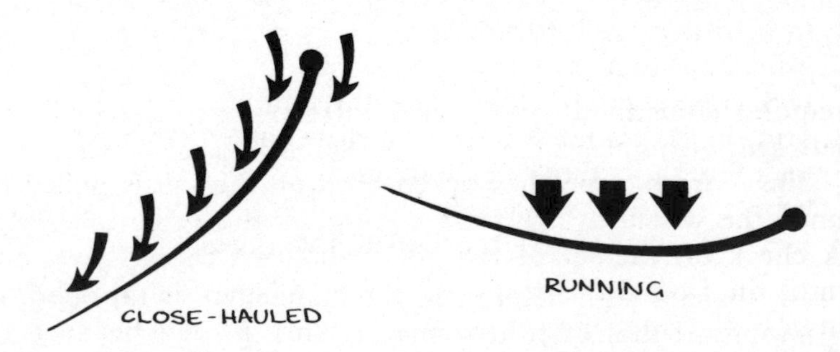

FIG. 15 Action of the wind on the sails

sails to carry out the manoeuvre. Pupils should be taught that, when making course changes towards the wind, sails must be pulled in and the centreboard lowered. The only exception to this is, of course, going about, when the mainsheet is left in its original position. As the process of going about speeds up, from a leisurely reach-to-reach to an active fetch-to-fetch, it is necessary to speed up the movement of the crew and helmsman. It is important that both should be in the centre of the boat as it passes through the wind. A special watch must be kept on the helmsman's foot position, especially from a fetch to a fetch. The Instructor should ensure that the sailing area is arranged in windward lanes for this session.

It will be found at this stage that pupils are very aware of their surroundings and are beginning to understand wind direction, having mastered basic course-changing skills. They have done the impossible, sailed against the wind. Now comes the time when they must learn to sail correctly using their powers of judgement and observation.

Session 8 – The Five Essentials

The boat is sailed to the sailing area, all previous sessions being revised. The Instructor demonstrates the following five essential points ensuring that they are included in all future sailing expeditions.

1. *Sail Setting*. Pupils should be reminded that sails act as deflector plates. The Instructor should demonstrate what happens when they are pulled in, or let out, too far.

Mainsail – from a weathercocked position, the sail is pulled in until it is obviously filled. Changing direction *into* the wind causes the sail to flap, indicating that it must be pulled in further. Changing direction *away* from the wind requires adjustment of the angle of the sail to the wind, by letting it out, until it flaps and pulling it in, until it sets.

Jib – from a weathercocked position the sail is pulled in until the whole of the front edge stops fluttering or lifting. A check on the set of the jib is obtained by letting it out until the front edge begins to flutter, after which it is pulled in until the fluttering stops.

2. *Balance* – the athwartships attitude of the boat. Normally

speaking the boat should be sailed upright. It is the crew's responsibility to balance the boat initially.

3. *Trim* – the fore-and-aft attitude of the boat. The helmsman is responsible for the correct trim by placing himself and the crew in the correct position. It varies as follows: Close-hauled, the majority of boats sail better with the weight slightly towards the front. Reaching and Running, the boat should be level, with the transom just clear of the water. When Planing, the weight should be towards the back, but constantly adjusted to keep the boat sailing as fast as it will go.

4. *Centreboard*. This is often the most neglected, and least understood, part of a sailing dinghy, yet it is one which most affects speed, pointing ability etc. The centreboard is there to stop the boat sliding sideways. It is shaped to create as little drag as possible. It always operates with water ap-

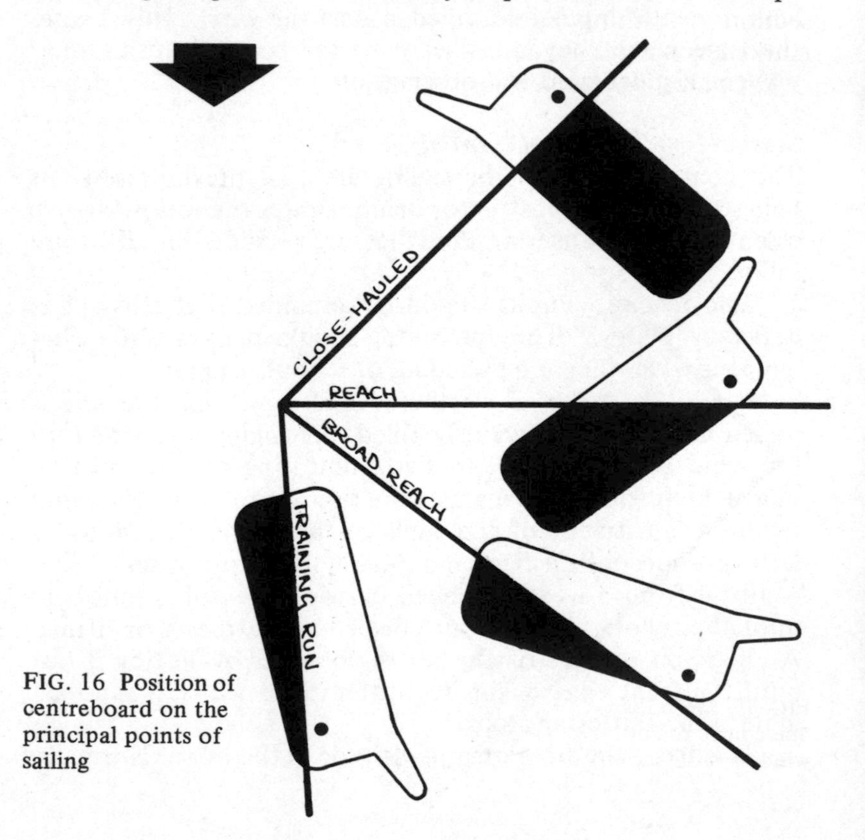

FIG. 16 Position of centreboard on the principal points of sailing

proaching the leading edge at an angle. On all points of sailing, there is an optimum position when the board or plate is counteracting sideways drift and generating lift to windward. The following recommendations are guides for training only. Much finer adjustments are required for the experienced helmsman: (i) Close-hauled – fully down. (ii) Close reach – three quarters down. (iii) Beam reach – half down. (iv) Broad reach – quarter down. (v) Training run, with only about six inches of the board protruding. (Fig. 16)

From a broad reach onwards, the centreboard acts as a skeg, providing directional stability. In strong wind conditions it is often wise to reduce board area to allow the boat to 'give' to the waves; on the reach, and run, slightly more board may be retained to increase lateral stability. The centreboard definitely falls into the trial-and-error section. Training boats should have the centreboard case marked as previously described.

5. *Course Sailed*. Pupils will take time to grasp the simple

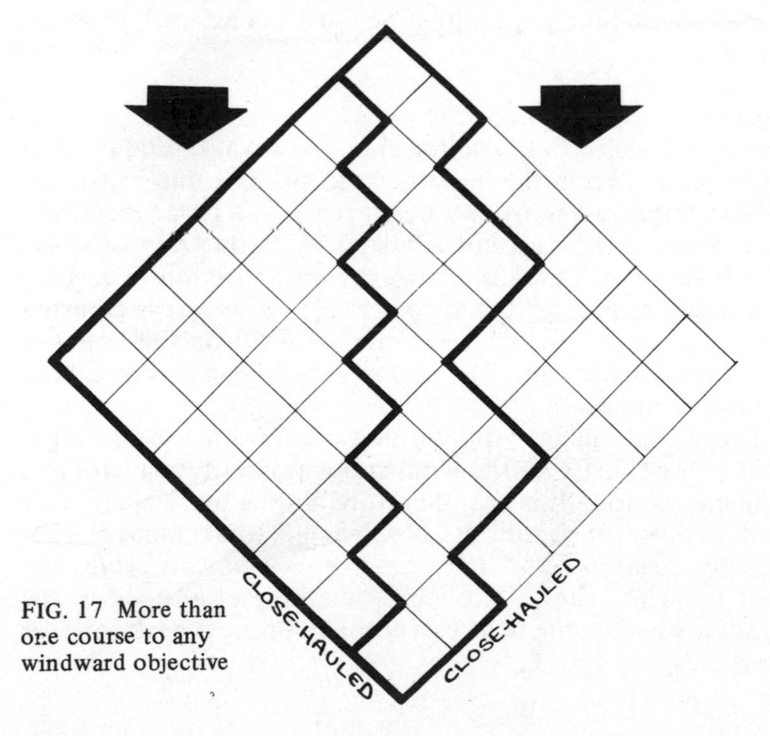

FIG. 17 More than one course to any windward objective

fact that there is more than one course to a windward point. Three simple variations are shown in Fig. 17. The best course is dictated by wind, tide and obstructions. Pupils must be encouraged to make decisions based on personal observation. It sometimes helps to devise a game based on the grid system of basic manoeuvres: Simple first steps to be replaced at a later date with more complicated manoeuvres and racing courses.

Teaching Points. If the Five Essentials are to be assimilated by pupils, constant revision is absolutely vital. As stated, they are a very basic concept, but an Instructor must revise, and enlarge, as pupils become confident.

Further information can be gained from yachting magazines and the many books which have been published. In this way, each pupil assimilates as much as is useful for his particular task or need. Sailing the boat on the jib luff is common practice, but it must be borne in mind that it is only valid when the jib itself is correctly trimmed and therefore, in a teaching situation, pupils must be taught constantly to adjust the sails.

Session 9 – Downwind Sailing

The boat is sailed to the sailing area. As always, total revision takes place. From the basic hove-to position the Instructor demonstrates sailing from a beam reach to a broad reach and then a run. The sails are adjusted by letting the rope out. The function of the sails changes from deflection to pushing as the boom reaches the shrouds. Crew weight is adjusted until a point is reached when the crew sits on the opposite side to the helmsman. The jib loses its driving power, except in very strong winds.

Downwind sailing is quieter and often warmer because the boat is travelling with the wind and waves, but the boat has a tendency to roll. It is not, therefore, a time for sleep, neither is it a time for failure to observe the wind, especially its velocity. *The force of the wind is not so obvious whilst the boat is on the run.* It can be something of a shock to the uninitiated when the boat is eventually brought back towards the wind.

Training Run. For training purposes the run is defined as being some five to ten degrees off a true dead run. Fortunately, it is possible to recognise when this position is reached, because of the action of the jib.

With the boat turning from a beam reach to a run, the jib should be watched closely. It will lose its drive and hang limply, then, just prior to the downwind position, it will flutter and move towards the windward side of the boat. The helmsman should centralise the tiller and bring the boat back to the position where the jib returns to the leeward side. It will be found that this course is then five to ten degrees from the run. It is a safe position in which to teach beginners, even in varying wind patterns. Each pupil practises sailing from a run to a reach; reach to a run; then from close-hauled to a run; run to close-hauled, until they *fully* demonstrate good boat control. The crew, meanwhile, is occupied in constantly adjusting sail and centreboard.

Teaching Points. The sailing area must be chosen carefully, and extra vigilance is required for the last part of the session, if the boat is being sailed in the vicinity of other boats which are practising the same exercise. Special attention must be paid to the mainsheet, which should not be drawn down over the back of the tiller hand, when making adjustments, otherwise the skin will become raw. At the end of the session, the Instructor should demonstrate a number of gybes to show the pupils that it is possible to change direction away from the wind. These need to be accompanied by only a brief explanation, and no attempt should be made to allow the pupils to gybe the boat, at this stage.

Session 10 – Gybing

The difference between going about and gybing is fundamental to a beginner. In going about, the boat moves beneath the stationary sail, giving the pupil time to gather his wits. In gybing, he finds the sail moving over the boat and his wits are quite likely to be scattered if he doesn't keep his head down!

The introduction of a set sequence for the gybe has triggered considerable discussion. The training gybe involves pulling in the mainsail prior to gybing and this has prompted observers, often of the casual variety, to condemn it because it induces the front of the boat to turn towards the wind. This situation should never arise when the pupil is under instruction because the sail can be reefed sufficiently to avoid it, and when the helmsman is practised the gybe is a quick fluid movement with the boat turning away from the wind as the sail is being pulled in.

The gybe is included in the teaching sequence at this stage, not because it is dangerous but because the pupils need a greater degree of skill and awareness to carry out this fast-moving manoeuvre.

Land Drill. The same props are used as for going about. The boat is assumed to be on a training run, boom out to (but not touching) the shrouds, tiller and mainsheet held correctly, centreboard for a training run. It often helps if pupils are taught to begin the land drill from a beam reach so that they have to describe how to find and then hold a training run with reference to a shore mark.

1. Helmsman checks boat and horizon, especially to leeward. When ready, he calls out 'Stand by to gybe'.
2. Crew checks around boat especially to leeward, answers 'Yes' if it is safe to gybe.
3. Helmsman pulls in sufficient mainsheet to bring the boom to a position about eighteen inches to two feet from the quarter, taking care to feed the surplus rope 'down the hole', pausing momentarily halfway through the adjustment to check the horizon, and to correct course.

Note: The exact position of the boom is not critical and depends upon the type of craft being used. The purpose of the adjustment is to induce a gybe soon after the turn away from the wind has been initiated, and to prevent rolling during the gybe induced by a sail which is allowed to set forward of the beam at its head.

4. At the end of the mainsheet adjustment the helmsman traps the mainsheet, does another check and calls out 'Gybe ho' pulling the tiller towards the body. Swivelling his trunk towards the stern the helmsman grasps the tiller

with his free hand, lifts the tiller hand free taking care to lift the mainsheet free of the folded tiller extension. The crew grasps the new mainsheet and prepares to move quickly across the boat.

5. As the boat turns away and through the wind the helmsman waits for the leech of the mainsail to fold, then moves to the centre as the boom swings across, centres the tiller as the boom crosses the centreline, and sits down on the new windward side.
6. As the pull comes on the mainsheet the helmsman lets out a bit at a time to apply the drive in a controlled manner. The crew sets the jib as required.

The turn is completed when the boat is steady on its new required course, both sails correctly set, boat trimmed and balanced.

Teaching Points. As for the previous land drill. Initially, pupils will find it difficult to complete step 5 in the short time available as the boom moves over the boat, but practice soon makes it a fluid movement. Experienced sailors will recognise that this is a very basic way of gybing. They are absolutely right – this is a very basic way of gybing. It must be appreciated that it was devised to enable the trainee to gybe the boat successfully whilst retaining complete control. Essentially it is a *method*, rather than a collection of 'good intentions and prayers', and it can be used in quite boisterous conditions. During the initial preparations for the gybe the boat must be kept on course. The gybe must not be attempted from a broad reach. Unlike going about when the pupil was a beginner and needed time to move about the boat, this manoeuvre has to be carried out at its natural pace.

The major teaching point is to ensure that the tiller is central as the boom swings over the boat. When the drive comes onto the sail the boat is driven in a straight line and should be between a training run and a broad reach.

During the gybe, lee-helm and weather-helm are experienced. The beginner will not wish to know, but later due allowance and correction must be made. After the gybe the mainsail should be let out to the correct running position.

Session 11 – Gybing (Afloat)
Before going afloat the Instructor should repeat the gybing land drill. The boat should be sailed to the sailing area by the pupil as a revision of Session 9. The Instructor should demonstrate the gybing sequence and sail the boat back to the windward end of the sailing area. Pupils practise the gybing sequence in turn, bringing the boat back to the starting point. In this way they are practically revising the sessions omitted at the start of the programme. The sailing area should permit pupils to complete six to eight gybes.

The crews have now completed the basic training and should be sufficiently skilled to undertake a solo sail before moving on to the next phase, which includes increasing the sail area, using the tiller extension and sitting out.

It is often a good idea to complete this phase of the course by setting a simple triangular course for the pupil to sail around whilst the Instructor supervises from a safety boat. This gives the Instructor an opportunity to assess each pupil's ability and to gauge whether they are ready for the next stage, or need additional tuition to complete the solo sail satisfactorily.

Many Instructors complete the first solo sail on the second day, but it is more usual for the pupils to reach it on the third day of a course; thereafter the rest of the week is spent in learning to use more sail, a tiller extension and 'sitting out' as well as all the seamanship skills which a novice sailor needs when sailing unsupervised.

Session 12 – Conversion to Full Sail
(using the tiller extension and sitting out)
Up to this point all sailing has been carried out with reefed sails, enabling the pupils to sit inboard and to use the tiller with the extension folded back and retained by a sail tie or rubber band.

As soon as full sail area is employed, the pupil must learn to use the tiller extension and to sit out. Whilst the basic RYA Method is designed to cater for the simplest situation, other equally effective programmes are based on the use of the tiller extension from the first sail. The National Sailing Centre, Cowes, has adopted such a system which is reproduced below to show how they approach the problem. It should be remembered that their staffing ratio and facilities enable a high degree of supervision and control to be exercised.

Tiller extensions are now much more reliable than they were even a few years ago; all use the universal swivel joint which permits the extension to pivot through a hemisphere. The extension is brought forward and around in both tacking and gybing.

For the land drill the chairs should be placed further apart to indicate the sitting-out position.

Going About

1. Helmsman sails boat with tiller extension, thumb on top. Mainsheet in forward hand.
2. Helmsman checks that mainsheet is 'down the hole', front foot forward.
3. Helmsman checks boat and horizon, calls 'Ready about', crew checks especially to windward and replies 'Yes'.
4. Helmsman, rope under thumb, checks to windward, calls 'Lee ho' and pushes tiller away. Crew releases jib, picks up new jib sheet.
5. When the boom reaches the quarter, helmsman moves towards centre, changes hands on the extension, placing thumb of free hand on top towards tiller and lifts mainsheet well clear.
6. Helmsman pushes tiller away some more and, facing aft, moves across the boat bringing the tiller extension around and forward, keeping the tiller pushed away. Sits on weather side as boom reaches quarter – checks horizon.
7. As sails fill on new tack, crew and helmsman reset sails.

Gybing

1. Helmsman steers boat on to training run – helmsman checks boat and horizon, especially to leeward, calls 'Stand by to gybe' – crew checks to leeward and replies 'Yes'.
2. Helmsman pulls in some mainsail, clipping it under the thumb, spare 'down the hole'. Places free hand on extension close to other hand, thumb on top towards tiller. Separates mainsheet outwards, calls 'Gybe ho'.

3. Moves to centre of boat taking extension round and forward to other side, pushes extension away to gybe.
4. Centres tiller when boom is overhead, sits down, letting out mainsheet. Helmsman and crew set sails and balance the boat.

Body Movement. We have already established that the basic foot position is in the centre of the boat. When sitting out, the helmsman's feet must be placed under the toe straps. The new sequence is as follows: as the helmsman moves outboard the front foot is kicked into the strap to ensure correct location, followed by the back foot. Whilst sitting out the helmsman's backside is outside the boat against the side of the boat, therefore proper adjustment to the toe straps is essential on all boats to suit each helmsman.

Teaching Points. During the land drill the helmsman must be taught to move his front foot first. The feet must be firmly placed in the straps. Toe straps often cause concern in training boats. (As they are not required during the earlier sessions, it may be necessary to devise a method for stowing them out of the way during this period.) The crew follows a similar procedure, except that, in very wide boats, an extra step may be needed to negotiate the centreboard casing.

Increased Sail Area. A pupil who has learned to sail with reduced sail area has concentrated on learning the basics of boat handling. Increasing the sail area will assist him to consolidate his knowledge and to become a competent novice. Sail should be increased to make the pupils' task interesting, rather than difficult. The increased speed warrants increased vigilance.

Additional Sessions (Rules of the Road)
For many pupils additional practical sailing sessions with an Instructor may never be necessary. *By the end of Session 12 the pupil should be a competent novice in the art of sailing a boat*. If he never takes an Instructor afloat again, his future sessions will be the years in which he gains experience. It is obviously not possible, within the pages of this book, to

discuss at length all the detailed items contained in the various syllabi of the dayboat certificates within the RYA National Proficiency Certificate Scheme.

During the course of practical instruction, many of the *theoretical* items will have been covered during instruction. However, since they are such an important part of being afloat, the very elementary and basic Rules of the Road, as they may relate to the sailing of dinghies in the early stages, are set out below:

In theory, power gives way to sail but in practice the sailor has to look after his own safety especially when operating in congested waters. Many power-boat owners do not understand the seemingly mindless antics of a sailing boat tacking up a channel and it is often wiser to adjust the tacks to sail behind or away from a motor cruiser. Commercial shipping has no option but to remain in a narrow channel, therefore the onus is on sailing craft to keep clear.

The rules governing sailing boats meeting are strictly observed and one is expected to react correctly.

Opposite Tacks. A boat which is on port tack (with the wind blowing over its port side) gives way to a starboard-tack boat (with the wind blowing over its starboard side).

Same Tacks. A boat which is to windward or is overtaking must keep clear of other boats.

One further rule which should be observed when navigating a channel is that traffic normally keeps to the right, and it is easier to move with the flow than against it.

CHAPTER TWO

The Structure and Management of a Training Programme

The main problem with sports which rely on complicated equipment is that much of the time is spent preparing or repairing that equipment. If sailing is not properly organised it can be a total waste of time, where the actual time period afloat is so short as to encourage the would-be participants to seek their adventure elsewhere. Even in a well-organised set-up, each pupil has to perform a certain number of functions before, during and after sailing (see Fig. 18).

Fig. 19A shows what happens when a group of people are taken sailing. Each of the functions experienced by the individual is complicated by numbers and the very presence of a group of people prolongs each stage.

Many new clubs and centres have benefited from advice

FIG. 18 The basic needs of a club sailor

FIG. 19A

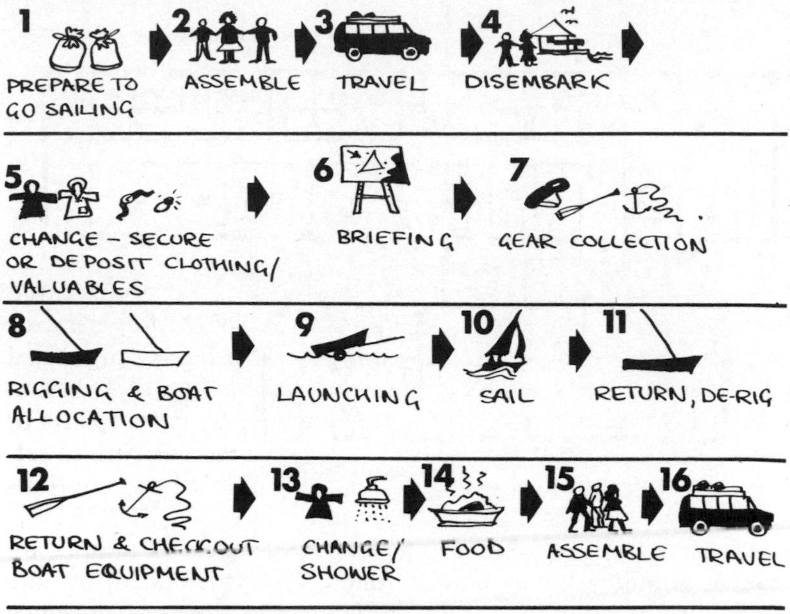

1 PREPARE TO GO SAILING
2 ASSEMBLE
3 TRAVEL
4 DISEMBARK

5 CHANGE – SECURE OR DEPOSIT CLOTHING/ VALUABLES
6 BRIEFING
7 GEAR COLLECTION

8 RIGGING & BOAT ALLOCATION
9 LAUNCHING
10 SAIL
11 RETURN, DE-RIG

12 RETURN & CHECK OUT BOAT EQUIPMENT
13 CHANGE/ SHOWER
14 FOOD
15 ASSEMBLE
16 TRAVEL

FIG. 19B

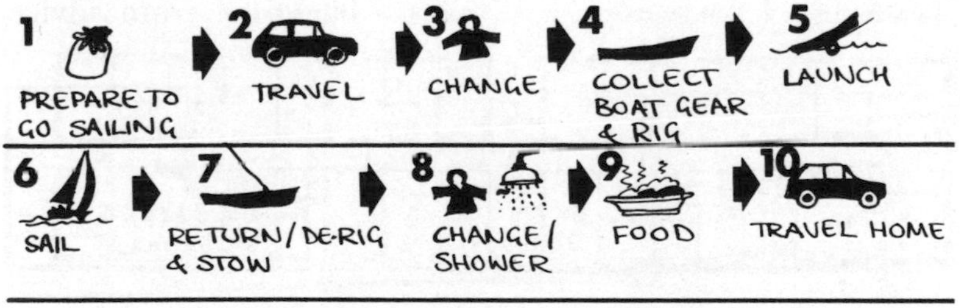

1 PREPARE TO GO SAILING
2 TRAVEL
3 CHANGE
4 COLLECT BOAT GEAR & RIG
5 LAUNCH

6 SAIL
7 RETURN/ DE-RIG & STOW
8 CHANGE/ SHOWER
9 FOOD
10 TRAVEL HOME

FIG. 19A-B Organised activities

given by RYA staff, but every Instructor should look carefully at his own teaching situation to see what improvements can be made to speed things up.

Fig. 19B shows a breakdown of the basic needs of club sailors who congregate at weekends. One of the worst aspects of club sailing is the design of changing facilities – clothing and valuables are liable to theft whilst crews are sailing, and wet crews returning from sailing tend to spread

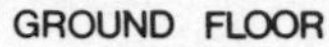

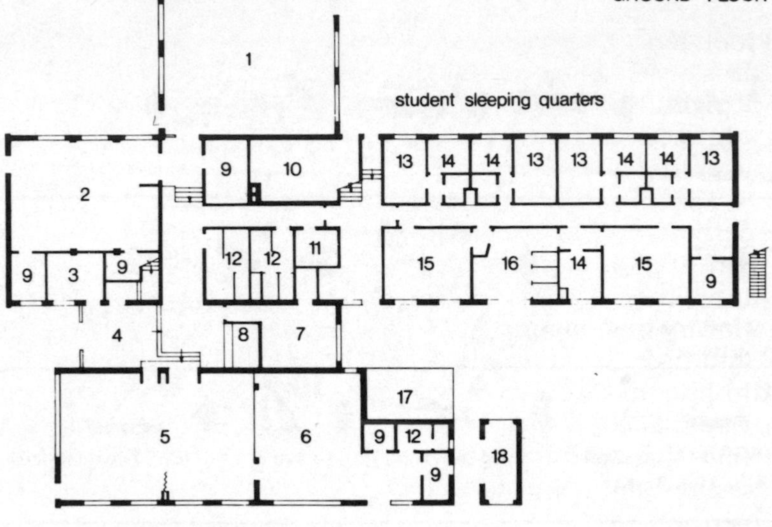

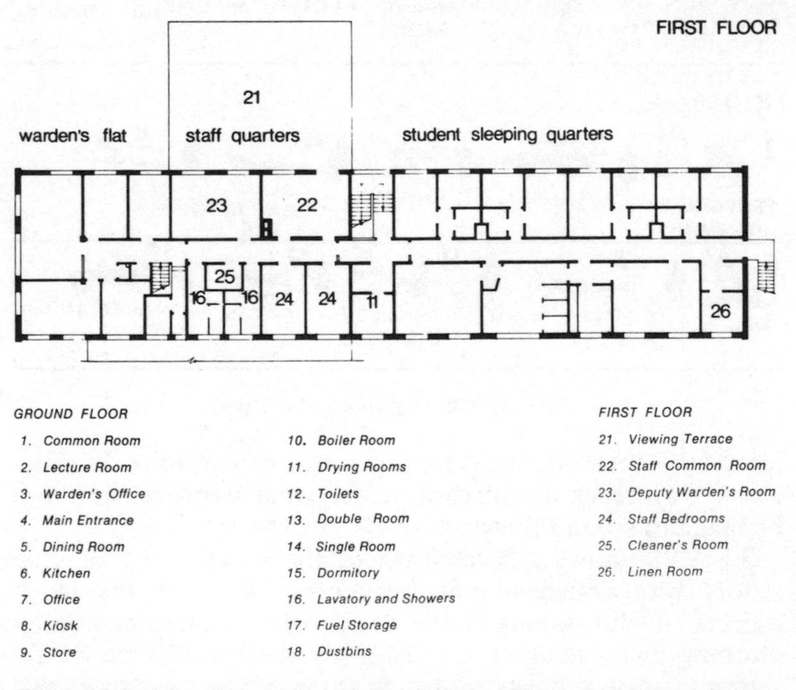

FIGS. 20 and 21 Floor plans of the Grafham Water Residential Centre

water over everything. With care a one-way system could be devised provided it incorporated a hot-air dryer – but usually a compromise has to be reached and people must use their common sense. The architect can help by building a floor which slopes gently towards the wet area thus helping to keep the dry area free of standing water.

Education centres which have a constant throughput of groups need a facility which can segregate each group for the period of their attendance. Provision must be made to safeguard and segregate clothing and belongings on the same principle used at sports centres, a central depository where clothing is placed on and in a special hanger, or a building with segregated duplicate changing areas. (Figures 20 and 21 show ground-floor and first-floor plans of the successful Grafham Water Residential Centre.) Once a reasonable system has been established to enable participants to ready themselves for sailing, a programme of instruction sees to it that they are profitably employed during their time at the teaching establishment, and that resident and visiting Instructors readily slot into the administrative arrangements.

Sailing programmes are dictated by the site – lake, river, estuary, open sea – as well as by the weather and tides. An example of a centre operating under seemingly difficult conditions is the National Sailing Centre at Cowes. It is situated on the commercial banks of the River Medina, adjacent to a shipyard and opposite a new marina. Direct access to the river is barred by the double rows of wooden mooring piles which in the sailing season are filled with boats with the exception of one opening. Upstream, the very tidal river offers good sailing only when the tide is in. Downstream, a veritable gauntlet of chain ferries, car ferries, hovercraft and hydrofoils must be run to reach the open sea off Cowes seafront, and even that is moving rapidly east or west most of the time. Yet with good management and supervision thousands of beginners have learned to sail at Cowes and, because of the variety of difficulties and hazards, have benefited from the concentrated experience.

Shoreside Facilities and Tuition

Sailing is all about getting afloat in boats and doing it, but

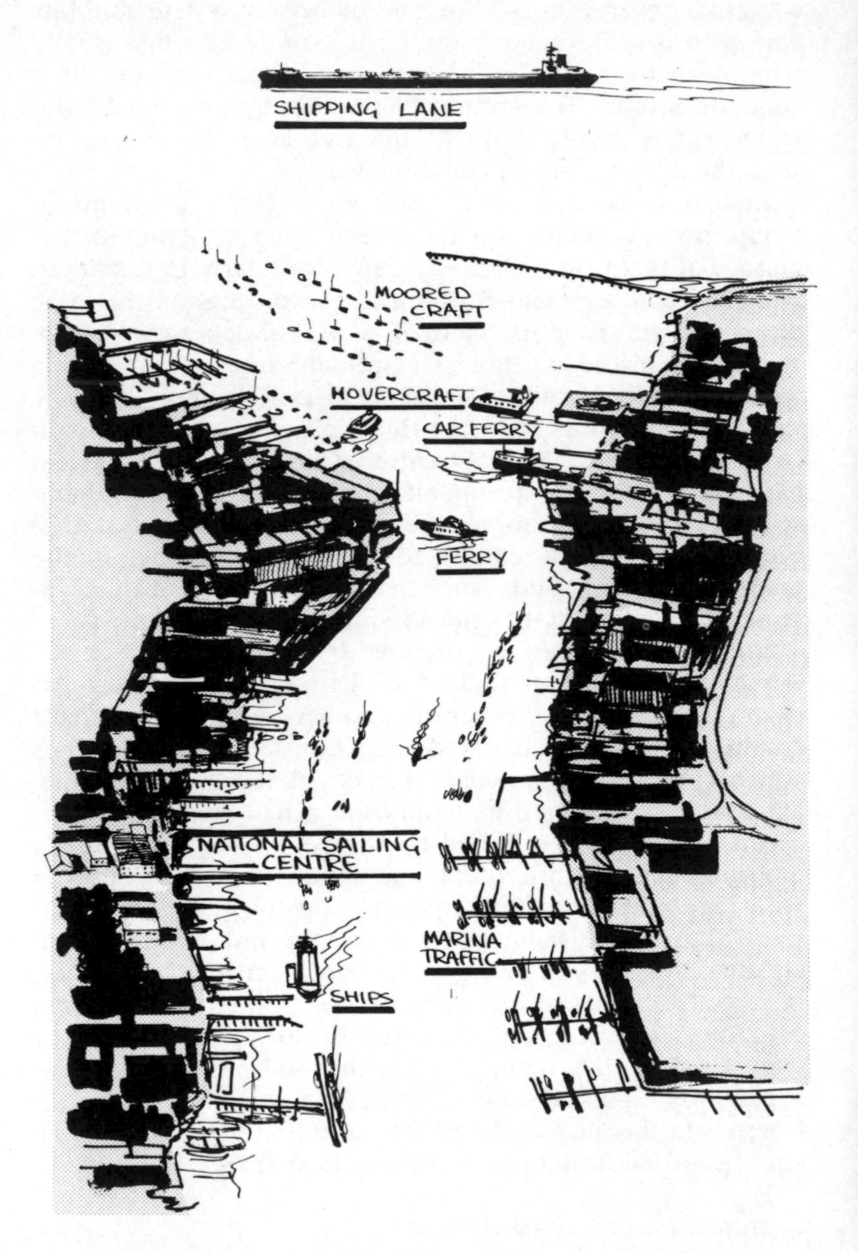

FIG. 22 Location of the National Sailing Centre at Cowes

shore-based facilities are needed for changing, storage and tuition. The onshore tuition complements work afloat.

The sailing programme will be limited by the numbers and types of boats and availability of staff. Once it has been decided what type of tuition can be offered, and the duration of each course, it is then necessary to decide what can reasonably be achieved in the time available.

The Teaching Method described in Chapter One relies heavily on work afloat, but it is quite obvious that there are going to be occasions when it is not possible to follow the sequence. Shore sessions can be very wasteful and depressing if not properly planned in advance. This is the time when most unqualified Instructors are of little use, and the burden falls upon the trained staff. The most difficult situation arises when sailing is impossible on the first day's session. This is too often the day for 'parts of the boat' from truck to rubbing strip. There are precious few Instructors, because of their wealth of experience, who can retain the rapt attention of their flock for an entire day or even session. Anyway, it's no way to teach a participatory sport, even with basic facilities.

The pupils must be introduced to the boats and the gear. They should be learning how to do useful tasks. If the whole day has to be spent ashore, the evening can, at least, be enlivened by films or slides. Perhaps a talk by a local yachting 'character', duly briefed to be entertaining, can be arranged.

During the day there is plenty to do. Start with the topography of the sailing area and a walk around the shore with a short visit to the local boat yard or sail loft. By the end of the course you will, in any event, have covered all the following list in detail. However, if the weather continues to hold you up, a great deal can be done on shore.

Safety – basic requirements – learning to wear lifejackets – water practice if the swimming pool is available or if the water is warm!

Basic bends and hitches – sufficient to secure a boat to a ring, a pole, a beam and an anchor, and of course the bowline.

The boat's gear – rudder, sails and ropes. It should be possible to rig a small boat indoors or undercover so that pupils will learn where each part goes. Some parts must be correctly named, but care must be taken not to become technical or to attempt to name everything.

Weather – it is often worth recording the early morning shipping forecast to use it as a basis for a study of the progress of the weather being experienced.

Handling boats on trolleys – correct stowage of boats and gear, emergency repairs.

Preparation of equipment – marks, ground tackle etc.

Safety and rescue boat handling – engine care, safety procedures.

It should be borne in mind that, to the seaman, bad weather days ashore are 'make-and-mend' days, memorable because of the feeling of security from the elements. A large group should be split up into groups of about six persons, so that everyone is working with a competent Instructor.

Shore sessions which occur later in the course can be used to enlarge upon work done and to introduce correct terminology and a little basic theory, which relates directly to skills already learned. Land drills may conveniently fit into an enforced shore session, in which case every effort should be made to perfect the technique being taught. Further work is possible along the following lines: boat handling, trim, balance, sail setting, rig tuning, hull finishes, centreboard and rudder profile sections, course made good, and tactics. If the pupils are attending a racing course, or advanced boat handling, the topics should be chosen to stimulate further thought, theories should be discussed, techniques analysed. The racing rules should be dealt with by discussing actual incidents – RYA appeals cases – using groups as protest committees. Each point and rule is explained as and when necessary. Tactics should be played out on the specially marked floor or board, or walked in a field.

All sessions ashore should have a purpose and should not be regarded as lost time.

Instruction Afloat

Assuming that a programme of instruction has been worked out to fit the times available afloat, there is still much to be done. Crews allocated to boats, Instructors to crews, and leaders to groups. A general safety briefing to all course members, specific briefings to Instructors, and safety and rescue boat handlers. All gear required must be loaded into boats, as must food and drink if the group is to be afloat all day. So much time can be wasted because of lack of planning and because crews or individuals have received insufficient briefing. Great emphasis must be placed on the smooth flow of people, equipment and boats, one-way systems, proper return of trolleys etc. Once afloat it may be possible to sail unimpeded to a well-defined area and begin sailing at once. But it often happens that the sailing area is situated beyond an area of moored boats, or down-stream, necessitating a planned assisted passage. A strong tidal stream may dictate that all boats should be towed, often a very efficient way of getting boats to a sailing area in one piece. If towing is envisaged, a specially made-up floating tow rope should be trailed. Boats either make fast with their own painter at the same time and with a rolling hitch, or pick up the pre-spliced painters attached to the rope. Whichever method is used, it should be possible for the dinghies to cast off immediately the order is given. This is not possible if a dinghy is tied directly to the tow-rope, hence the pre-spliced painters which allow the end to be secured inboard. All boats used for training, particularly, should have substantial through-bolted towing cleats.

Whatever pupils are doing the person in charge acts as a shepherd and watch-dog. Strays are rounded up, casualties collected, and a careful watch is kept for shipping and weather changes. If a boat must return to base, it should be accompanied, otherwise the boat should be anchored and the crew taken ashore by high-speed rescue boat.

If 'casualties' are cold they should be handed over to the shore staff to ensure that they shower and warm up.

Organisation afloat relies heavily upon the person in charge. His aim should be to secure the maximum amount of benefit and enjoyment for his pupils, and to return them to the base with sufficient time to pack boats and equipment away, change and shower.

Long-Term Planning

Day to day, or week to week, planning is closely related to

local conditions. A *yearly* training programme is quite a different matter, because it has to take into consideration the winter months. Either all forms of sailing activities cease, or the training programme is continued. If it is continued, it must be planned down to the last detail, or it will fail. During the last few years, it has been possible to sail right up to the end of November. It is becoming obvious that, if the mild autumns continue, this period should be utilised as part of a much better organised annual programme, commencing in September. This coincides with the end of the club racing season and the beginning of school term and evening institutes. Programmes should, if possible, commence with practical sessions, so that, when sailing is no longer possible, the shore sessions will continue smoothly.

By the spring, it will be possible to commence race training. Course members should be ready to join in club racing by the end of the season. After a season's sailing or racing, the following autumn can be used for *special* racing and boat-handling courses.

The National Proficiency Certificate Scheme, with its attendant Log-book, is easily adapted to the suggested annual programme commencing in September. It should be possible to award the Elementary Certificates in the autumn, assuming that it is possible to have twelve full evening sessions and three full week-ends. Much, however, depends on the actual teaching time afloat, but a well-conducted programme would also include special periods of preparation for the Instructors.

The Coaching Scheme, being the responsibility of the Coaches, will, as a result, be more highly organised at course level. Special care will still be needed, at area and regional level, to ensure that programmes are prepared at least a year in advance. A complete regional programme should be published well in advance and communicated to all sailing clubs, schools and interested groups. The area and regional policy will be a balance between proficiency and coaching, to ensure that sufficient qualified people are eligible to be trained as Instructors, and that there are sufficient Instructors to meet the demands on sailors who wish to improve their sailing.

Coping With Large Groups
It is accepted that pupils attending courses following the day-boat syllabus will benefit from the Instructor/pupil ratio set out in Chapter One. There are many occasions however where through accident or by design the ideal ratio is not possible and a large group of would-be sailors find themselves with one Instructor. Many sailing schools offering holiday courses are faced with this situation, often without the benefit of a trained Instructor.

The prime consideration is safety and the person in charge of sailing must determine whether the experience or inexperience of a particular Instructor or helper is sufficient to cope with the anticipated situations which are bound to occur, especially if the group is made up of total beginners. An Instructor faced with a group of beginners is in a 'crowd control' situation and must accept that instruction must give way to supervision.

Obviously, the RYA does not condone such a situation especially when fee-paying students are involved, but neither can it bury its head in the sand and hope it will go away; therefore research has been carried out into ways and means of catering for larger groups under the guidance of one Instructor. The research programme owes much to the generosity of an anonymous benefactor who donated twenty-four Topper dinghies to the RYA, to be used in trailers of six boats by youth organisations and sailing clubs.

Group Teaching Using One-Man Dinghies
The programme is based on the assumption that one Instructor is equipped with a safety boat and six Topper dinghies. The programme of instruction is based on the RYA Teaching Method but with certain essential modifications as follows.

The briefing on rigging, launching and recovery is more detailed. All pupils must demonstrate that they can name, rig and stow each part of the boat and can reef whilst afloat (usually practised with the boats ashore on a grassy area), and know what to do in the event of a capsize.

The Instructor demonstrates launching and sailing away from the launching site and sails a set course previously drawn out for the pupils with detailed explanations. Such a course will usually comprise a shallow figure-of-eight reaching course around two buoys placed about one hundred metres apart.

Prior to the first sail each pupil will demonstrate an understanding of the 'going about' manoeuvre with particular emphasis on the importance of the boom as an indicator (once again the land drills can be carried out with the pupils sitting in their own boats as a group, following the instructions given by the Instructor).

Other essential information relates to stopping by letting the sails flap; getting out of a head-to-wind situation by sailing backwards with the tiller pushed towards the boom; and making the boat move forward from a hove-to position by pulling in the sail and the tiller.

Converts to the Method will by this time have thrown their hands up in horror at this complete reversal of approach – talking about sailing before doing it! But if the person who is learning to sail is the only person in the boat then he/she must have some idea of what to do once afloat.

Headmaster Ron Highcock of the Norfolk Schools Sailing Association pioneered the multi-pupil approach with his Junior School pupils and their Optimist dinghies. Using Filby Broad, the majority of instruction is carried out from a floating pontoon situated at the centre of a circle of buoys. The children learn a story about a dog on a lead – boom and mainsheet; a gate – the tiller; and a bull in a field – the sails and with shouted words of guidance and encouragement learn to sail in two days!

Once afloat in the Toppers our original group are controlled in the same way, by signal or by voice, and one of their first tasks is to practise coming alongside the anchored safety boat for further instructions. They progress from reaching figure-of-eight course directly to a gybing course and once this and a successful capsize/recovery have been mastered, the Instructor can begin to extend the programme to include follow-my-leader tasks and an introductory race programme. We have found that pupils learn much faster in one-man boats and need to have a much more detailed programme to keep them fully occupied once they have mastered the basic skills.

There is still considerable discussion relating to capsize/

recovery in the programme. My own view is that it could come in the first session if the air and water temperatures permit, but that it fits quite nicely into the period when the pupil has gained the confidence of both tacking and gybing. Prior to this each pupil must rely upon the capsize briefing given in the introductory session.

If it is not possible to utilise a number of small one-man boats, the Instructor must train a few helmsmen who will then sail the available boats with novice crews as passengers. If the group attend on a regular basis, the Instructor will be able to spend some time with each member of the group. There is much to recommend bringing in additional Instructors at the start of a course to give everyone a chance of individual tuition.

Visual Aids

The best visual aids are the boats and their equipment. When this manual was first published it was anticipated that the current interest in visual aids would continue and that fairly sophisticated visual aids would become available wherever sailing was taught. The present situation shows that whilst many sailing schools and education centres have 16-mm film projectors, overhead projectors, film strip and slide machines, many others don't even have an electricity supply! The greatest need is to cater for the worst situation with wall charts, then to move into film strips which can be cut up to make slides, then have film projectors and overhead projectors.

The simplest form of mobile permanent aid is the well-prepared flip chart which can be hung over a rail, and of course the black and increasingly white boards allow the Instructor complete freedom from a classroom situation.

Visual aids must be used to advantage, to introduce or reinforce concepts – they should never usurp the Instructor or deprive the pupil of the opportunity of experiencing a particular sensation. The aim must be to use the visual aids to pass on to our pupils our enthusiasm, knowledge and expertise.

Films and Slides. After considerable discussion the RYA, in conjunction with BP, produced two films – The RYA Method,

Part I and Part II, covering most aspects of the teaching method. This direct approach gives the pupils the opportunity to see a training programme in stages and is a good aid to learning. The danger is that some Instructors may be tempted to use the film rather than their own teaching skills.

A good film is an excellent way to project or arouse enthusiasm and also to convey information. Most of the films at present available on sailing are background material rather than an effort to project a teaching point. They are nevertheless valuable in providing this background and can play their part in a planned course of instruction. They stimulate interest and discussion. Most films will benefit from being 'introduced', by a brief talk on their particular value or aim. But if the aim is purely enjoyment, then say so!

The use of films has to be planned well in advance. There is often difficulty in obtaining copies from suppliers and last-minute requests are doomed to failure. The RYA booklet on films is a good basic starting point for the keen Instructor.

Most clubs, schools and other teaching establishments possess or have access to a projector. If buying a new one, the type with a stop/pause button is preferable for the teaching situation, as the film can then be stopped and the Instructor can enlarge upon, praise or condemn a particular point. To make a film to satisfy the particular needs of an area, programme or scheme is ideal, but costly.

Slides are a more easily acquired visual aid. Again it should be possible for most Instructors to obtain the use of a slide projector. The burden of establishing a collection of suitable slides, however, falls on the individual. It should not be impossible for an individual or group of Instructors within an authority or institution to make their own collection of teaching slides. The Method can be recorded in this way. A 35-mm camera is the most economical way of producing slides, copies can be made so that more than one set is available in an area. Teachers' centres and resources departments of large educational establishments often have the means for reproducing copies of slides at very reasonable prices and, if approached, would in most cases be willing to help.

Slides have the added advantage that the Instructor can make his own commentary to suit the needs of the particular group. A very useful addition to teaching materials is a collection of slides concerned with local cloud studies to be used in conjunction with basic and, indeed, advanced lectures on 'weather'.

Tapes, to be used in conjunction with slides, are also a valuable aid. These can be prepared by the Instructor.

Pictorial Charts. Some wall charts are available from the RYA Seamanship Foundation. Apart from being wall decorations they have the advantage of always being there, if there is a place for permanent displays! Charts of knots, weather, classes and types of boats, flags, codes, buoys, etc, are really not difficult to obtain, or even to make!

Apparatus. Models, preferably home-made for cheapness, the ubiquitous 'broom handle and piece of flex' for the Method; boats for race starts illustration; the eternal assistant, the blackboard, all help in the task of instruction.

The teaching of rope work, knots, etc, particularly benefits from visual assistance. Construct a knot display board, using contrasting colours of rope, to remain in permanent display, with spare ropes fixed by the side so that pupils may practise their knots in spare moments.

Video-Tape. This method of recording a sailing practice session and then showing the recording in the 'recap' land session is indeed an excellent way to correct unknown or unbelieved faults in techniques! It has many obvious advantages; its main disadvantage is its cost, and its dislike of salt water!

Overhead Projectors. Like all expensive mechanical instruments, the overhead projector is very useful when lecturing if the Instructor has access to one. It has the advantage that material can be prepared and stored in advance, either on the roller or on prepared slides.

CHAPTER THREE

Safety

As with all other things in life, it is possible to have too much of a good thing. If safety is over-emphasised, the beginner is either intimidated or overwhelmed, and as a result does not get the most out of his sailing. It is important to note that people who have been involved in sailing accidents either benefit from the lessons learned, or take up a land-based sport!

Safety is an attitude of mind which embraces individuals, groups, and craft. There should never be a need to treat it as anything other than a normal precaution, similar to that which involves, say, checking that the bungs are in the boat.

Too many people come forward to make excuses for not wearing proper lifejackets or for leaving them off for this or that reason. They must make their own decisions concerning their own groups, but in the event of a drowning, a verdict of negligence would be far more appropriate than that of 'death by misadventure'. So, when training beginners the attitude of the Instructor is obvious and needs no statement.

Lifejackets

It is not sufficient to rely on a person's own ability to keep afloat, merely because he can swim. After much experiment, a suitable lifejacket has been designed, which is acceptable to canoeists and sailors alike, and which conforms to British Standards BS 3595. There have been, and may be in the future, other standards, but this one, in its basic form, has thirteen and a half pounds of permanent buoyancy and can be inflated to thirty-five pounds. In its deflated state it can be worn over the normal trapeze harness without interfering with the crews' ability to trapeze correctly and comfortably, and is very suitable for the purposes of small-boat sailors.

It goes without saying that a lifejacket must be worn

correctly each time it is donned; this constitutes a basic safety check. Some lifejackets have patent fastenings, others are fastened with tapes. Whichever method is used it is important that it can be released in an emergency.

An uninflated lifejacket with thirteen and a half pounds of permanent buoyancy will give a swimmer sufficient support to permit him to carry out any work involved in the righting of a boat. In its fully inflated state it will float him in a safe position, even if he is unconscious.

Some lifejackets have no permanent buoyancy and are inflated either by a CO^2 cylinder, or by mouth inflation. A few are specially designed as constant-wear lifejackets and are often worn by those who have to wear a lifejacket throughout the sailing season.

Individuals should be permitted every opportunity to practise swimming in their lifejackets. One important factor, which will emerge, is that it is necessary to swim on the back with fully inflated lifejackets, and that it is not easy to climb into the boat unless the jacket is partially deflated.

Buoyancy Aids

There are a number of buoyancy aids on the market which are described as vests or jackets. Crews of racing dinghies must decide which suits their purpose best.

Clothing

Clothing is equally a consideration of safety. If a person is not correctly equipped for the anticipated conditions, or even unexpected or prolonged conditions, he may well suffer from the effects of cold. This may in turn lead to a lessening of awareness and eventually to a misjudgement.

Much depends on the sailing area and the proposed duration of the sail. The golden rule is to encourage beginners to put on too much, so that garments may be discarded whilst sailing. It is fairly safe to assume that our climate will seldom encourage the pupil to discard anything!

The wearing of wet suits for winter sailing has prompted a theory that they should also be worn during the summer months. This may be fine for those who sail for short periods, but for extended sailing it is much more sensible to wear warm clothing, protected by waterproofs. Incidentally, the wearing of wet suits alone, although they do provide *some* buoyancy, is not sufficient for total safety.

The best warm clothing should contain natural wool, and it should not be too tight. Dinghy sailors are not noted for their elegant clothes. In fact, some have a distinctly 'rag-and-bone-man' appearance. However, most sailors soon get to know what suits them best. Waterproof clothing poses a much greater problem, because whilst waterproof garments certainly do not allow water in, they unfortunately also prevent perspiration from escaping! The wearer therefore gets wet from within and may be just as uncomfortable on a hot day.

Most waterproof garments are made from synthetic materials bonded to a rubber or plastic backing. The seams of the garments are either 'doped' or taped. The cut of the garment is important, the fewer seams the better. Seals at wrists and ankles seldom prevent water trickling in. Zips should be plastic covered and need to be greased lightly. An important secondary function of outer clothing should be to prevent heat loss caused by wind chill. One-piece suits are popular with some racing crews, but the majority of dinghy sailors prefer separate trousers and jackets, thus obtaining a valuable overlap in the centre of their body, and ventilation when the jacket is open.

Newcomers to sailing are often horrified to find that they must walk into the water when launching and recovering boats. Wet feet create considerable problems afloat and it is for this reason that beginners should be warned about trying to keep their feet dry. Some form of foot covering should be worn at all times. Many people have taken to wearing calf-length neoprene socks with oversize sailing shoes; others improvise by wearing woollen socks covered with plastic bags, held in place by rubber bands. Knee-length sailing boots are ideal for shallow water.

If a week's sailing is undertaken, the neck should be protected from chafing with a scarf or towel, which also doubles as a water trap.

Head covering: hats range from Victorian 'straws' to woolly bobble caps. The important consideration is that, in sunny weather, the wearer is protected from sunstroke and, in cold weather, that his head is protected from heat loss.

In wet weather, the hoods of sailing jackets provide some protection, but often obstruct vision when the wearer turns his head.

Gloves: a few years ago, gloves were almost unheard of in sailing dinghies. Today almost every top crew-man wears them to protect his hands from the ravages of tightly-wound, constantly played, spinnaker sheets. Such gloves are made from leather and are expensive. Cotton gloves are cheaper and just as effective for less demanding boats. A week's sailing can play havoc with hands not used to the normal wear and tear afloat.

Individual Boat Safety

Individual boat safety is often neglected. It entails ensuring that proper safety checks are carried out before going afloat, and that the correct equipment is aboard. Much will depend on local conditions. A boat sailing on an enclosed reservoir will always drift ashore, therefore it could be argued that an anchor is not as essential as a pair of oars. A boat sailing from an estuary will need a good anchor of the 'plough' type with a warp equal to, at least, three times the maximum depth of water. Flares and oars are essential, if the boat is to sail alone. The list is very large, but the message is simple – be prepared for the normal emergencies of sailing. It is as well to bear in mind that most of the things likely to be needed can be stored safely in the ubiquitous plastic bucket, which must of course be attached to the boat with a rope!

Individual boat safety extends to the crew, who should know what action to take in emergencies.

Group Safety

Whenever groups of boats go afloat, it is important that the leader of the group makes a number of plans to cater for various contingencies. Normally, a safety boat will be in attendance and will control the group by flag or sound signals. The flags and shapes used by the fleets affiliated to the Association of Solent Boatwork Bases are shown in Fig. 23. When very large fleets are afloat at the same time, they

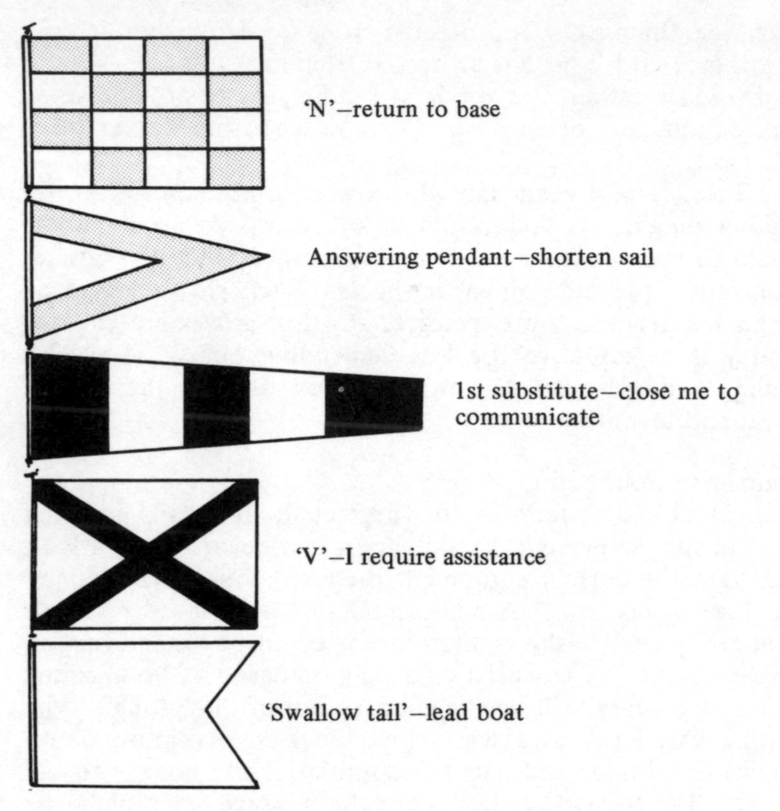

FIG. 23 Solent Boatwork Bases' flags

should be split up into small units, each with a leader. They should know their sailing area or objective and also the areas which are *not* to be sailed in – main shipping lanes, shallows, etc.

It is essential that all skippers are briefed before going afloat, and that groups are dispatched from, and to, base as complete units.

Most trouble occurs when crews are being taught to use spinnakers and trapezes. The exhilaration causes a complete disregard of pre-arranged areas. In training situations, time afloat is very valuable. Pupils will benefit most from a controlled teaching situation, in which they have a responsibility to themselves and others.

As sailing venues become more congested, many groups

use distinctive coloured sails for quick identification of their craft.

Boat Design

It is generally accepted that the majority of training boats will be standard stock designs. Each area has its own particular requirements or prefers a particular craft. Three typical examples of all-purpose craft are the Yachting World GP14, the Bosun and the Wayfarer. They are totally different in design concept, yet fulfil the requirement of being both a satisfactory initial trainer, with reduced sail, and a lively performer under full sail.

The use of GRP is now almost universal. Since the majority

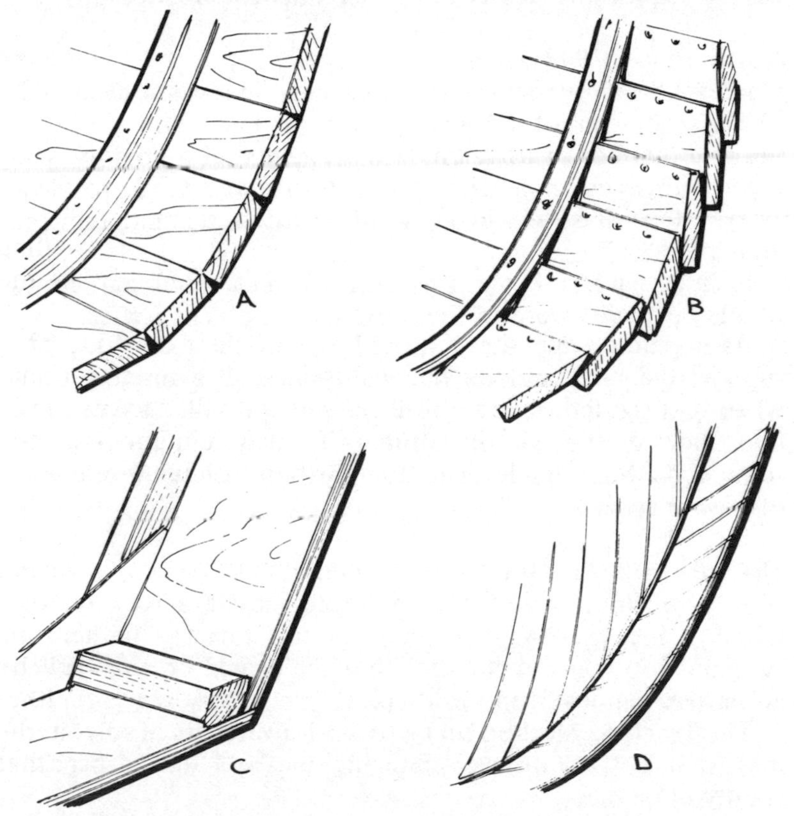

FIG. 24 Boat-building methods: A–carvel; B–clinker; C–ply-chine; D–cold-moulded

of teaching boats are used constantly for twenty-six weeks a year, it is important to regard the bottoms of GRP boats as being very vulnerable. Many boats have moulded keels and bilge keels, which soon wear through. They should be protected with quarter-inch-thick strips of hardwood, which should be fixed with a modern two-part adhesive.

When checking GRP boats, particular attention should be paid to centreboard cases and side tanks, which are bonded to the main shell. Constant straining often causes the joints to fracture, thus rendering the boat unsafe.

Traditional boat-building methods include carvel, clinker, plywood and cold-moulded construction (Fig. 24). Repairs usually require the services of an experienced boatman.

Distribution of Buoyancy

Whatever the construction, the boat must float when swamped. The distribution of buoyancy is most important. Fig 25 shows a number of different arrangements. If a boat has too much buoyancy, it is difficult to board, and tends to blow away. If it has too little, it fills with water and remains immersed.

Each design has its own problems when capsized, and crews should be made aware of the more serious eccentricities.

As a general rule there should be sufficient buoyancy to support the boat and its occupants in such a manner that, when it is righted, it may be baled out and sailed away. The buoyancy should be distributed in such a manner as to support the boat in a level attitude, without undue immersion of bow or stern.

THE WEATHER AND BASIC WEATHER SYSTEMS

This is without doubt the least predictable safety factor. Given a nice sunny day, most groups manage to get by (without too many incidents!) but the arrival of a disturbed air pattern can lead to untold epics!

The Teaching Method seeks to teach awareness of surroundings; the sky and its ever-changing contents should be constantly observed.

There are many excellent publications which set out in detail the interpretation of clouds and weather forecasts.

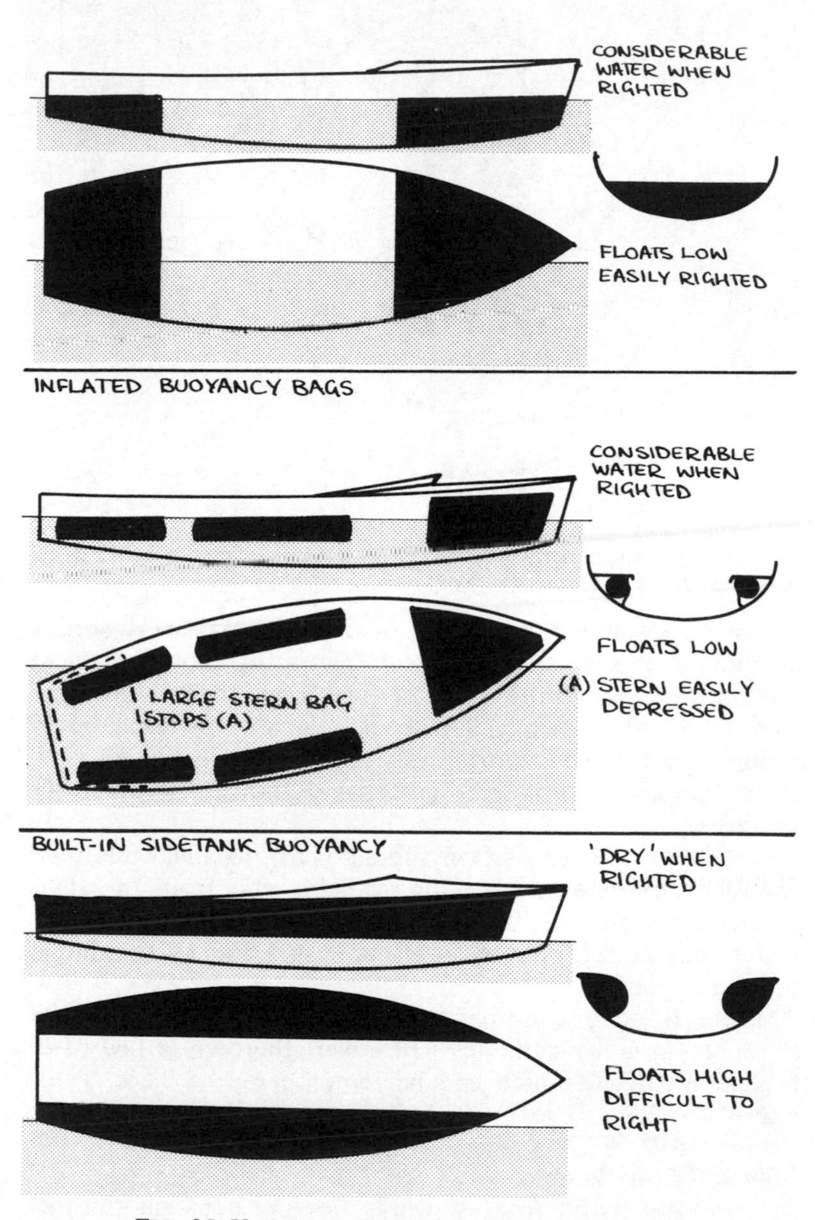

FIG. 25 Various methods of distributing buoyancy

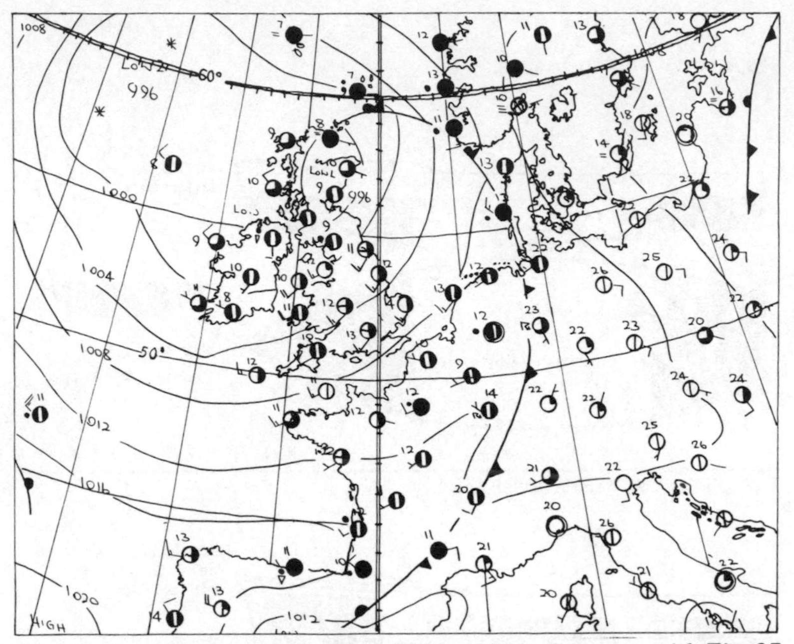

FIG. 26 Synoptic chart: 18.00 hrs, 23 May 1979. Compare with Fig. 27 (*Courtesy H. M. Stationery Office*)

Those responsible for safety should always use every source at their disposal. A competent Instructor should make it his business to ensure that he has consulted all available sources of information. These include Met Office national reports, and local reports, especially from RAF stations. Even annual records can give some indication of likely patterns.

In addition, every sailor should learn to make his own forecast from the information available and from the signs in the sky; many a local fisherman has a fund of knowledge which may be acquired by pupils or Instructors by the simple process of asking!

There is no one simple explanation of weather, because there are so many variables. However, there are a few basic factors involved, which can be remembered as basic 'yardsticks'.

High and Low Pressure Areas

Because the world rotates, winds flowing between the differing pressures are deflected and disturbed and, combined

FIG. 27 'Tiros N' satellite picture: 15.00 hrs, 23 May 1979
(*Courtesy H. M. Stationery Office*)

with upper air patterns of faster moving jet streams, give northern and southern latitudes a considerable mixture of high and low pressure air systems.

The principal cause of low pressure is that air is heated and rises, leaving a gap. Once the air has risen it cools and is deposited as heavy air – high pressure. As the warm air rises, the surrounding air rushes in to fill the gap, and as cold air descends, it displaces warmer air – so a natural airflow is established between high pressure and low pressure areas. This would be fine if the globe stood still, but its rotation sets up turning forces in each air mass which then detach themselves and can be regarded as vortices similar to those created by bathwater running out the waste pipe, or as large gear wheels meshing with each other. High pressure areas rotate clockwise and can be likened to a screw being tightened – heavy air descending; low pressure areas rotate anticlockwise, a screw being withdrawn – lighter rising air.

Figs. 26 and 27 show a simplified chart of the systems over Europe and the British Isles on 23 May 1979 and a representation of the satellite photograph which backs up the forecast. Clearly visible is the junction between the cold air mass to the north-west of the British Isles and the warm air mass to the south-east of France. The junction of warm and cold air produces precipitation and the unstable air of the cold air mass indicated by the speckles gives thundery outbreaks of rain. Satellite photographs are increasingly used by television forecasters and are a valuable aid to formulating your own opinion.

For those who do not have access to weather charts, it is a case of either 'back to the sea-weed' or learn to interpret the signs of the sky. Every area of the British Isles has its own weather lore, with its associated rhymes and sayings. These should be put to the test, because many are surprisingly accurate.

Observation and Interpretation

For our purposes, the dinghy sailor can be regarded as being static; weather systems will therefore pass over him. If he were cruising he would pass through the systems.

We have to accept that, because weather systems have existed for millions of years, they will be complicated. The basic system shown in Fig. 27 has become distorted and influenced by the fact that, because of the tilted axis of the earth, the areas of high and low pressure are constantly advancing and retreating with the seasons.

Moving air can be likened to water in a stream. It has a basic directional flow with associated eddies and whirlpools. Land masses cause disturbances similar to those caused by the uneven bed of a stream. When cold water meets an area of warmer water, it flows underneath it and very little mixing takes place. Air acts in the same way.

If all air had similar properties, it would not be possible to distinguish the boundaries of the warm and cold air masses. Fortunately various factors help to give us visual clues. Water vapour, for example, is present in varying quantities dependent upon its origin. Air masses which have travelled over the sea – maritime air – usually pick up considerable quantities of moisture. Those which have travelled over land – continental air – are usually much drier. Both types take on the temperature characteristic of the land, or sea, over which they have passed. This is expressed as either tropical or polar. Fig. 28 shows the principal air masses which affect the British Isles.

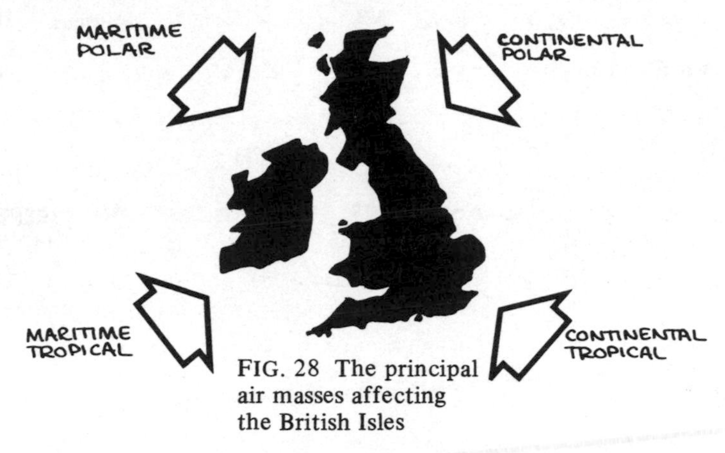

FIG. 28 The principal air masses affecting the British Isles

The air temperature decreases as it moves further from the earth's surface. The average rate is 10°C for every 1,000 metres. On a local scale this results in air, which has been heated at the earth's surface, rising until it reaches a point where it is cool enough to condense and form water droplets. These are visible in the form of clouds. A similar thing happens on a three-dimensional scale when dissimilar air masses meet. It will be appreciated that water droplets, which continue to rise, will eventually become ice crystals and that the resulting clouds will have a different appearance.

Clouds

Clouds (Fig. 29), like weather systems, are complicated. The sky often contains many types, each with its own individual characteristics.

To add to the confusion, clouds can have both Latin and English names. Only the basic cloud names are given here.

Perhaps the most easily identified clouds are the cumulus – the cotton-wool clouds of many a primary school landscape; the cirrus – the 'mares tails' of the upper sky; and the stratus – the layer of cloud which moves, blanket-like, shutting out the sun.

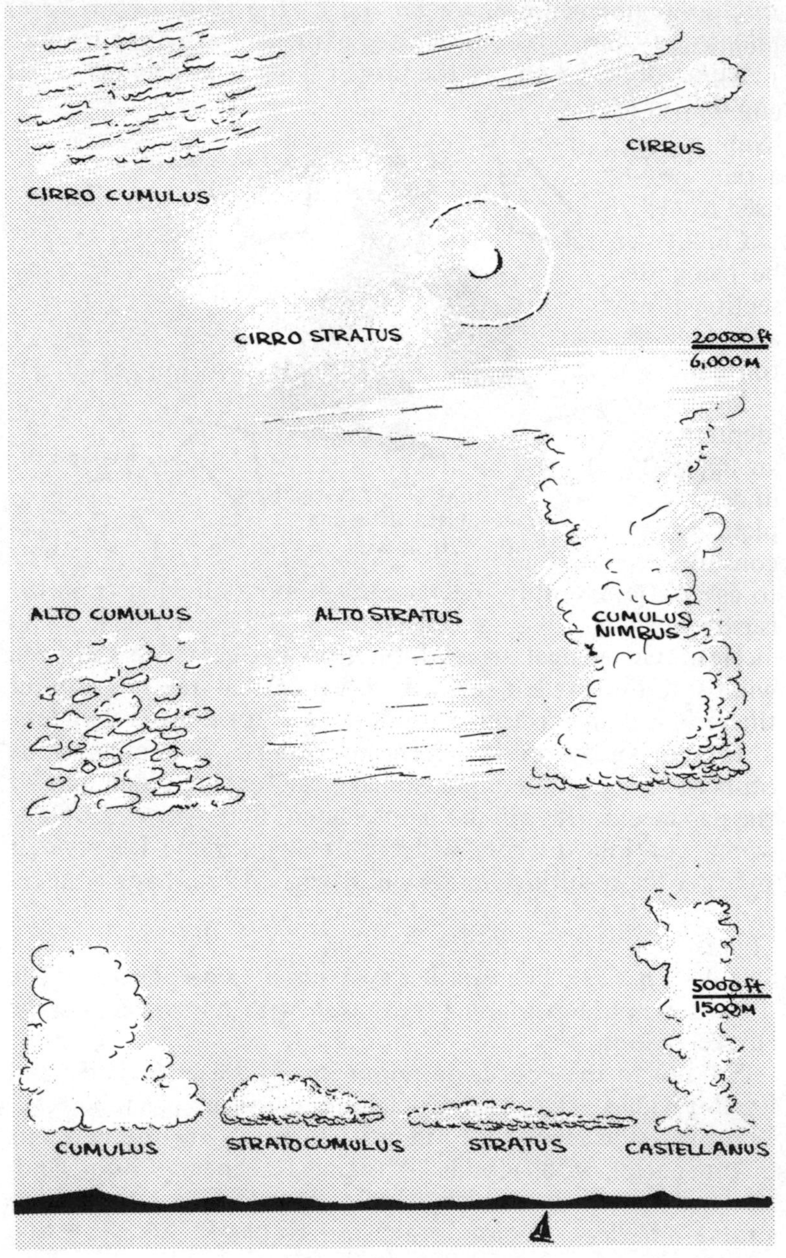

FIG. 29 Cloud types

Stratus and cumulus can occur at any height, and so are identifiable by height: alto-cumulus, cirro-stratus, etc.

When a large 'up welling' of air takes place, a much bigger cumulus cloud is formed and may be called cumulo-nimbus. 'Nimbo' or 'nimbus' is commonly used to indicate that it is a rain cloud. 'Anvil' – 'castellanus' and 'pilaus' are words used to describe the appearance of a cloud.

Cloud identification is essential if weather patterns are to be recognised from cloud sequences. Fig. 30 shows a cross-section through a 'depression' with its warm and cold fronts, and their associated clouds. The system is moving from left to right.

Most people in the British Isles know something about 'depressions' and that cirrus or 'mares tails' usually indicate an approaching frontal system. But the only way really to understand a 'typical' system is to observe and log the complete cycle of events, bearing in mind that it is essential to consult the weather maps of TV, Newspaper and Met Office to ascertain the exact track of the depression. This exercise is extremely valuable with groups who have time to spare.

Measuring instruments for temperature, humidity and wind speed are readily obtainable or may be constructed by the group.

In addition to the interpretation of the observations, the observer will gain valuable experience in gauging the speed of the passage of the depression.

FIG. 30 A cross-section through a depression

Local Weather Patterns
General weather patterns can be affected by the topography and each sailing site will have peculiar weather conditions. It is the responsibility of the Instructor to document local patterns and to advise pupils of the signs which signal good or bad variations.

FIRST AID

First aid is exactly what it says – the first attempt to preserve the life of a person who has suffered an accident prior to the victim receiving professional medical aid. Instructions given to non-medical persons should be simple and effective. Action in emergency should be swift, decisive and correct; indecision could result in death. Any action on the part of a first aider should be directed towards making a casualty comfortable, keeping him warm, preventing further injury and keeping him alive until further help arrives.

If an accident takes place afloat or miles from the nearest telephone, the medical aid must be more thorough. If the casualty has to be moved overland, a stretcher can be fashioned from oars or spars and sails. The main requirement is that the casualty is supported on a suitably padded firm baseboard which can be carried by two people.

Accidents on boats are usually confined to cuts, crushing and bangs on the head. Accidents around boats, especially when lifting, are to the back, the groin and the legs and feet. Accidents when fitting out and repairing, especially when handling paints and modern glues, are to the eyes and hands.

First-aid Boxes. As well as the obvious supply of bandages, plasters and slings, the first-aid box should contain scissors and tweezers, an eye bath and an eyewash solution suitable for counteracting acids.

Cuts. By far the most common accident and usually easily treated by holding the cut together with pressure until blood clotting stops the bleeding. The cut should be cleaned with fresh water and covered with a dressing. If the patient continues to work a waterproof plaster should be used. Deep wounds or punctured arteries or veins are more serious.

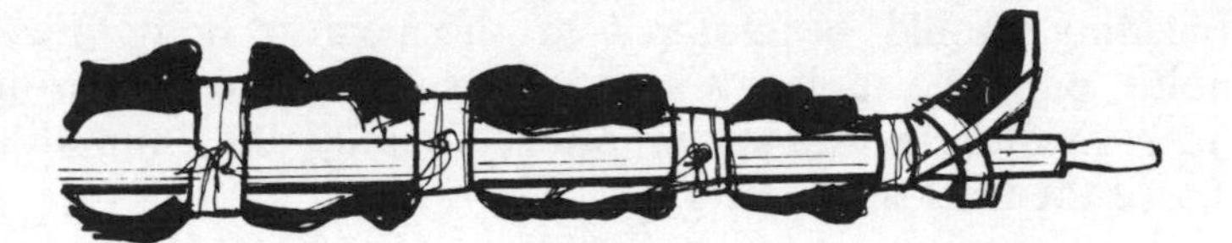

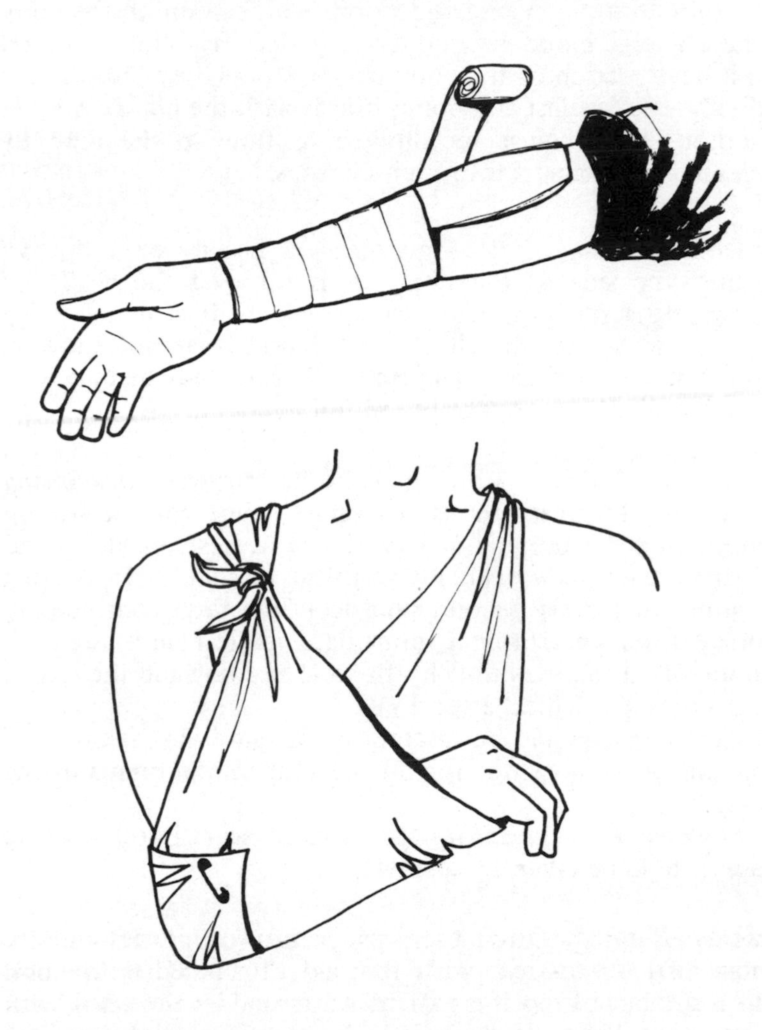

FIG. 31 Basic principles of bandage application–with splints (top); to hold dressings in place (centre); and as a sling (bottom)

Bleeding should be stopped at the nearest body pressure point, or by the application of a pressure pad over the wound. Seek medical assistance at once, keeping the injured area above the level of the heart.

Pressure Points. A pressure point is a position on the body where a large blood vessel crosses a bone. The flow of blood to a large section of the body can be stopped by pressing the blood vessel against the bone, but as with the old tourniquet method, blood must be allowed to flow to the limb by releasing the pressure every ten minutes.

Internal Bleeding. If someone falls heavily or is thrown against the side of the boat, or is hit over the head and shows signs of continued stress, seek medical help. Keep the victim warm and check that blood does not show in vomit mucus or urine. Damage to the skull may be indicated by a bleeding nose, ears or bloodshot eyes.

Burns and Scalds. More likely to be met with on cruising boats but the treatment is the same – put out the fire by smothering the burning area with the nearest towel etc and dissipate the heat with liberal quantities of cold water, bearing in mind that every second you delay the flesh continues to cook. If the skin is broken, immediate medical aid is essential. Shock often follows burns by fire and scalding and the victim needs prompt medical attention.

Acid burns should be treated in the same way, taking care that the water does not spread the acid to other parts of the body.

Sunburn is as dangerous as a fire or scald burn – severe cases should be taken to hospital.

Broken Bones. Often the most painful of injuries and the most difficult to treat with first aid. If immediate medical aid is available keep the patient warm and let the ambulance men move him. If he has to be moved, splint the limb without making any attempt to 'fix' the break, and prop the patient up in the least painful position.

EMERGENCY RESUSCITATION

Most people can give some first-aid assistance in most instances and get by, but this *does not apply* to resuscitating a person who has stopped breathing. The first aider must know what to do when and for how long.

The basic philosophy of 'get in there and blow' is an important one, because there are records of persons having died because by-standers did not think they could administer any form of emergency resuscitation. As with other emergency drills, the Instructor should always bear in mind that he could well be the recipient in the event of an accident. It is important that all members of a sailing group should know what to do if someone stops breathing. Even basic instruction will encourage a person to 'have a go'. He could save a life!

The lungs and heart are contained within the rib cage. The lungs transfer oxygen to the blood. The heart pumps the blood round the body. Air enters the lungs via the nose or, if that is obstructed, the mouth. It then passes down the pharynx, the common pathway for food and air, and is directed into the windpipe and the lungs. Food is prevented from entering the windpipe by a flap, the epiglottis. Once in the lungs, the air is dispersed to millions of little air sacs which extract the oxygen. Carbon dioxide is transferred from the blood to the air sacs and breathed out.

The lungs are activated by the diaphragm, the strong lens-shaped muscle attached to the spine and lower ribs. When it contracts, it lowers the bottom of the chest cavity and the ribs move up and out. These actions result in air being drawn into the lungs. The action of breathing is initiated by accumulation of carbon dioxide triggering nerve impulses in the respiratory centre of the brain. Asphyxia or suffocation occurs when air does not enter the lungs. This is often due to the tongue of an unconscious person falling back and blocking the pharynx or, in the case of the apparently drowned, by water blocking the air passages. Breathing can also stop, or be restricted, after an over-dose of drugs or an electric shock. Sometimes the heart is stopped as well. This is known as cardiac arrest. Within minutes the brain will be damaged due to lack of oxygen, therefore immediate action is essential.

As soon as the victim is reached, air should be blown into the lungs. It may be necessary to remove obstructions from the mouth or throat. If this is the case, the nose should be used. Seconds lost at this stage are a matter of life and death.

The casualty's head should be held higher than his stomach, to prevent vomiting. Any tight clothing should be loosened. Resuscitation efforts should be continued for at least half an hour, or until recovery takes place. Effective resuscitation is indicated by a return to normal colour of the lips, ears and face. If no colour change takes place, then cardiac arrest should be suspected. This will be confirmed by dilated pupils or lack of a pulse. External cardiac compression must be started immediately.

Notes. It must be stressed that the operator should be trained to carry out correct cardiac compression. However, it should also be borne in mind that a life is at stake, therefore cardiac compression should be attempted by anyone who knows the basic principles involved, *if no qualified person* is available to help.

A person who resumes normal breathing should be watched carefully until medical help arrives. It is also necessary to bear in mind that treatment for shock and/or exposure may be necessary.

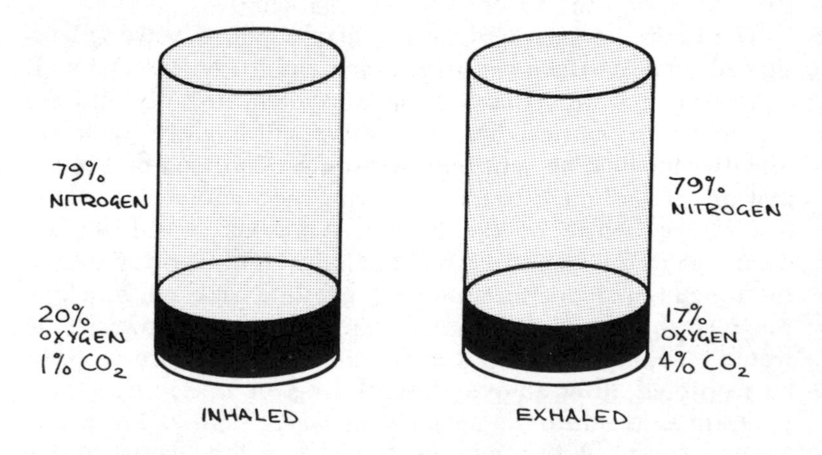

FIG. 32 The composition of inhaled and exhaled air

Expired Air Resuscitation

The most widely taught method is the 'expired air' method, when the operator breathes into the victim's mouth or nose and relies on gravity to push the exhaust gases out when he stops. Expired air resuscitation is accepted as being the most effective method. It can be carried out by a single operator, working under the most difficult conditions. It is easily taught, and can be practised by children. When the casualty is on land the operating position permits external cardiac compression to be carried out as well.

Some people mistakenly believe that expired air is made up of carbon dioxide. Fig. 32 shows the composition of inhaled and exhaled air. It will be immediately obvious that there is only a slight reduction in the oxygen content of expired air.

Method. When breathing has stopped, action is necessary. The instructions given below are for ideal conditions, but nothing should interfere with getting air into the lungs.

First, lay the casualty on his back, with his head higher than his feet. Then tilt his head back, and lift and pull down the jaw. This should move the tongue away from the throat and open the airway (Fig. 33).

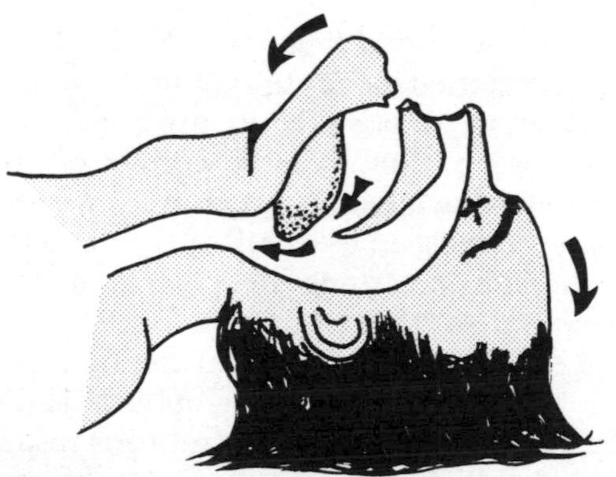

FIG. 33 Tilting the head back should clear the airways

If the casualty does not start to breathe normally:

1. Check the mouth and throat for obstructions.
2. Clear obstructions with fingers, or turn the casualty over and slap between the shoulder blades.

3. If obstructions cannot be removed quickly, don't waste time.
4. Check that the head is in the correct position.
5. Take a deep breath.
6. Close the mouth, and blow firmly but gently into the nose; or pinch the nose, and blow firmly but gently into the mouth. If the chest does not rise, there is still an obstruction. It *must* be cleared.
7. Turn your head away, taking another breath. The chest will fall.
8. Four quick breaths should be used to start with, thereafter the rate should be twelve times a minute.

Notes:

(a) *If the casualty is a baby*, breathe over mouth and nose with a puff of the cheeks. Repeat twenty to twenty-five times a minute.

(b) *Vomiting* – Turn the victim away, on to his side, clear the mouth and throat, and continue resuscitation through the nose or through a handkerchief.

(c) *Air in the stomach* – This can be detected by a swelling stomach. Turn the victim away, press gently on the stomach.

Demonstration and Practice. Expired air resuscitation should not be practised on anything but a training 'manikin' or mask. However, it is possible to use a partner to learn the basic operating position, and the correct positioning of the hands. The following advice is taken from *Emergency Resuscitation*, which is published by the Royal Lifesaving Society:

1. Practise breathing deeply, in and out, at five-second intervals.
2. Learn to put the head in the right position, by practising with a partner. Close his mouth and support his jaw by placing your thumb and forefinger respectively down either side of the jaw bone; curl your other fingers and fit the knuckle of your second finger under his jaw. Make sure that your curled fingers do not press on the throat.
3. Get used to adopting the correct position for the operator, by kneeling close beside your partner.

If dinghies are not tied down, this can be the result. (*Photo:* RYA)

Self-rescue – after the scoop method has been tried twice, it may be necessary to lower the mainsail if the boat is blown over. (*Photo:* Suzi Walker)

Left: The Mirror dinghy, ideal for learning to sail and for racing. Tightening the kicking strap would eliminate the twist on the leach of the mainsail. (*Photo:* Arthur Sidey)

Below: International Optimist dinghies, the ultimate in simplicity and enjoyment for young sailors. (*Photo:* Denis Merlin)

Right: These Topper dinghies are part of the RYA's fleet which can be hired by clubs at a nominal charge. (*Photo:* RYA)

Below: International Lasers and 420s racing in light airs. These two classes are sailed in the IYRU World Youth Championships. (*Photo:* RYA)

420

OPPOSITE PAGE
Above: The National Youth Squad preparing for the world championships.(*Photo:* Yachting World) *Below:* Constant spinnaker drills improve their performance. (*Photo:* RYA)

THIS PAGE
Right: 470s, Weymouth, 1978 – if you want to win you have to be on the line at the start. (*Photo:* RYA)

Below. Lasers – match racing improves close covering skills. (*Photo:* David Cruse)

Trapezing *Above:* Crew comes inboard prior to tacking. Note comfortable trapeze belt and position of trapeze handle. (*Photo:* RYA) *Below:* Just after the start of a training session; boat needs to be more upright. (*Photo:* RYA)

Instructing *Right:* The Drascombe Longboat is ideal for schools and youth organisations. Lifejackets should be worn – rather than left stowed in the lockers. (*Photo:* Yachting World) *Below:* It doesn't matter what type of boat you use providing the instruction is organised. (*Photo:* Yachting World)

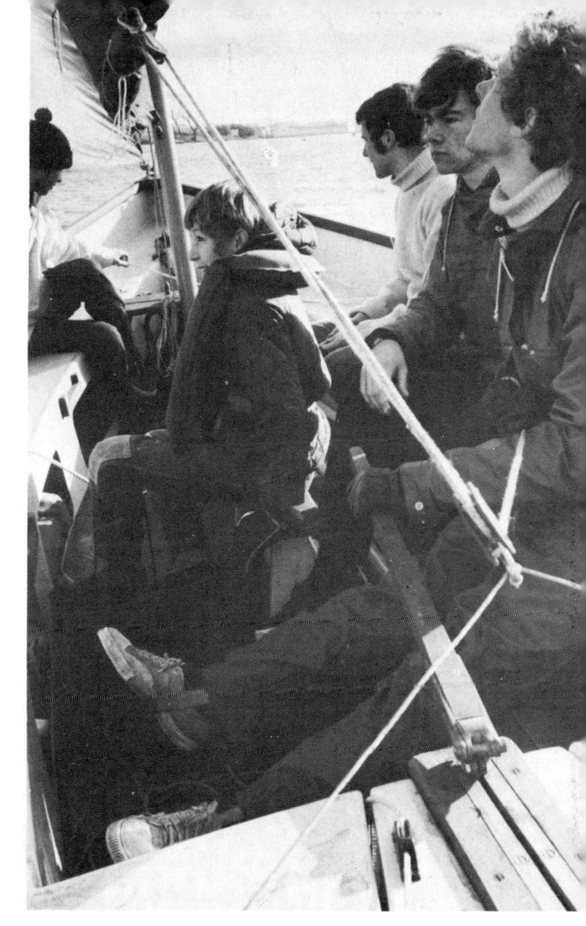

Instructing *Above:* With the dinghy in the basic hove-to position an Instructor gives advice to a helmsman. (Note reefing strop.) (*Photo:* RYA) *Below:* Using a high-speed inflatable this group of Instructors checks out an advanced certificate group. (*Photo:* RYA)

4. Take every chance of practising on a training manikin or a mask.
5. For practice and demonstration purposes, where a training aid is not available, lean over your partner and breathe down past his far cheek.
6. Practise turning your partner from his front to his back, to position him for resuscitation. Kneel by his side, stretch out the arm nearest to you, and grasp his far shoulder with one hand and his hip with the other, at the same time clamping his wrist. With a steady pull with both arms, roll him over against your thighs. Lower him gently to the ground, supporting his head and shoulders as you do so. Then replace his other arm by his side.

The Silvester-Brosch Method of Resuscitation

This method should only be used if, for any reason, the expired air method can not be used:

1. Lay the casualty on his back and quickly place suitable padding under the shoulder blades if immediately available. This padding should be thick enough to raise the shoulders so that the head just rests on the ground, with the neck extended to open the airway.
2. Check for any obvious restriction or obstruction, and keep the airway clear throughout.
3. Kneel on one knee just clear of the top of the casualty's head and to one side. Place the other foot beside his shoulder.
4. Grasp the casualty's wrists and cross them over the lower edge of his breast bone.
5. To compress the lungs, rock the weight of your trunk forward with straight arms until they are vertical, exerting a smooth, evenly-increased pressure.
6. Rock back, releasing the pressure and move back with a semi-circular sweep parallel to the ground until the casualty's arms are extended above his head. Stop when slight resistance is felt and do not force the casualty's arms to the ground in the extended position. Watch for the chest cage to lift as the extended position is reached.
7. Return the arms along the same route and place them in the original position on the casualty's chest ready for the

next compression. The whole cycle should take about five seconds. One second for compression, two for extending the arms, two for their return.

External Cardiac Compression

This action is very important if, during resuscitation, it has been ascertained that the heart has stopped beating. The usual signs of cessation of heartbeat include:

(a) No improvement in casualty's colour after five inflations nor any other sign that ventilation is proving effective.

(b) No discernible pulse.

(c) The pupils of the eyes are wildly dilated and do not react to light.

Method. Cardiac compression should be combined with expired air resuscitation:

1. With the casualty on a firm surface continue expired air resuscitation.
2. Kneel or stand by the side of the casualty. Thump the chest over the heart smartly with the ball of the hand. This may cause the heart to start.
3. If there is no response, begin regular compression whilst continuing to ventilate the lungs.
4. Place the heel of one hand on the lower half of the breast bone, keeping the fingers off the chest. Place the other hand on top in a 'mirrored' position, keeping the arms straight.
5. Rock forward until the arms are vertical and compress the breast bone squeezing the heart against the vertebral column. Release the pressure and repeat at the rate of one compression per second.

   In an unconscious adult the breast bone should be compressed a maximum of one and a half inches. Apply pressure with caution in the initial compressions. The normal operating pressure for adults is fifty-five to seventy pounds. (Practise with the bathroom scales to gauge the pressure).

   For children up to ten years, the pressure of one hand is sufficient. The compression rate should be eighty or ninety a minute.

Pressure should be firm, controlled and applied vertically. Erratic or violent action is dangerous. Six effective compressions will produce a pulse beat, reduce the pupils in size and improve the casualty's colour.

6. Compression should be continued until a regular pulse is felt or qualified medical help arrives.
7. Compression should be stopped when the heart is restarted.

Notes:
Combined external cardiac compression, with expired air resuscitation. A single operator should kneel beside the casualty and apply one inflation between each five to eight compressions. Two operators allow for one to give the inflation and to check the pulse and pupils and for the other to apply compressions at the same ratio as above.

Demonstration and Practice. The correct hand position may be demonstrated using a pupil, but on no account should pressure be brought to bear on the chest.

After Care. It is not sufficient merely to start the heart beating or to initiate breathing. The casualty may be unconscious, almost certainly he will be shocked and cold. An unconscious or vomiting casualty should be placed in the coma position (Fig. 34) until he can be handed over to trained medical staff. The casualty's airways should always be kept clear.

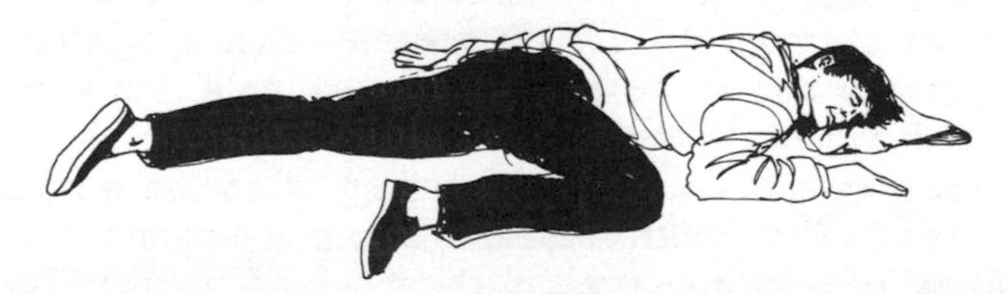

FIG. 34 Place an unconscious person in the 'coma' position

Water in the Lungs
It is important that all cases of apparent drowning are taken to hospital at the earliest possible opportunity. A specific

request should be made to the hospital authorities to check the patient for water in the lungs. Recent research has shown that *any* water, salt or fresh, damages the delicate tissues and can lead to the sudden collapse of a patient, many hours after his apparent recovery.

Shock

This is a distressed state caused by an insufficient supply of blood to the brain, brought about by severe loss of blood, nervous reaction which concentrates the blood in the internal blood vessels, acute medical and surgical conditions (eg heart attacks, etc), pain, exhaustion or infection.

In cases of shock due to severe loss of blood a transfusion will be necessary. General treatment should include:

1. Comfort and reassure.
2. Stop any bleeding.
3. Loosen tight clothing.
4. Insulate the body from the ground and prevent further heat loss.
5. Lay the casualty in a coma position if unconscious or vomiting, or on his back.

Cold can complicate an already dangerous situation. Every effort should be made to remove all wet clothing, dry the casualty and then to warm him, with clothing from rescuers, or by the use of blankets, sails, etc.

Hypothermia

For many years it has been accepted that not all persons lost at sea were drowned. It was assumed that in winter there was a greater risk because the water was cold, but very little informed evidence was available.

Those associated with the teaching of sailing were somewhat shocked to learn that even in mid-summer a person *could* die of exposure even in the English Channel. Against this background, the advice of the medical profession was sought. Professor Bill Keatinge of the London Hospital Medical School and Surgeon Commander Duncan Walters, RN of the Institute of Naval Medicine have both studied this subject for many years and have published their findings.

Professor Keatinge's research has revealed that many people who die after boating accidents die as a result of cold. Sometimes because the cold water causes drowning, sometimes simply because of the cooling of the body. Laboratory experiments showed that much depended on the individual, but that simple measures could do a great deal of good. For instance, a lot of clothing helps to prevent heat loss. Keeping still in the water conserves energy and heat. It is interesting to note that these findings are contrary to the normally accepted practice of discarding clothing and 'swimming to keep warm'.

Other factors which emerged were that warm water is easier to swim through than the more viscous cold water, and that, in very cold water, even the most competent of swimmers becomes weak, confused, lethargic and disorientated. Even a good swimmer may well collapse after swimming only twenty yards. It also happens that, when a person is dropped into cold water, reflex action causes him to gasp. If the sea is rough, it is possible that water may be inhaled, and result in panic. Immersion causes a shock to the nervous system, which may affect breathing for some minutes.

Surgeon Commander Walters' contribution to the RYA magazine in 1970 so clearly states the facts that it is set out in this book. The article was aptly titled 'Cold Can Kill'!

> 'To remain physically and mentally healthy and efficient the human body must be kept at a temperature very close to 36.8°C (98.4°F). It is, of course the *core* of the body which must be controlled in this way and not the more superficial tissues, such as skin, which may differ from the core temperature by several degrees. If the core temperature of the body should rise too high, death from hyperpyrexia (heat-stroke) will occur, whilst if the temperature drops beyond a certain point, then hypothermia will be the cause of death. A certain amount of variation in body temperature can, however, be tolerated without danger and it is usual for the deep body temperature to fall to 35°C (95°F) before hypothermia has actually to be diagnosed.
>
> 'The temperature-regulating mechanism of the body

is remarkably efficient and can maintain constant body temperature under widely different climatic conditions. The body has a highly effective sweating system which enables the amount of heat lost by evaporation in hot climates to be quantitatively controlled. "Automatic" constriction or dilation of the blood vessels at the surface of the body enables more or less heat to be conducted, convected or radiated away (according to need) and the metabolic system can markedly increase heat production within the body by adjustment of diet and the amount of muscular activity performed by the individual.

'In some climates, notably tropical, it is possible to maintain body temperature at the required level by these means alone. In colder regions it is usually necessary to augment them by the use of clothes, central heating etc. However, it should be remembered that, with the exception of specially heated garments, clothes serve only as an insulating layer between the body and the external environment, thus enabling the body to conserve the heat produced by its own metabolism. Clothes do not actually warm the body, they merely reduce heat losses from it and enable a thermal equilibrium to be achieved between the body and the environment. If this equilibrium is upset and the body is unable to maintain heat production at a rate sufficient to offset heat loss, hypothermia is the inevitable result. Clearly, the rate of heat loss, influenced by the heat production of the body, the insulation offered by clothing and the cooling power of the environment, determines the time required to develop hypothermia.

'In the open air, at low temperatures, the cooling effect of the environment is due to the combined influence of air temperature and air movement. It is common knowledge, of course, that wind has a very important effect on subjective sensations of cold.

'Air is not a particularly good conductor of heat. By trapping air between fibres, clothing provides heat insulation and, because this air is trapped, a layer of air surrounds the body, forming what may be called a "micro-climate". Anything which tends to remove

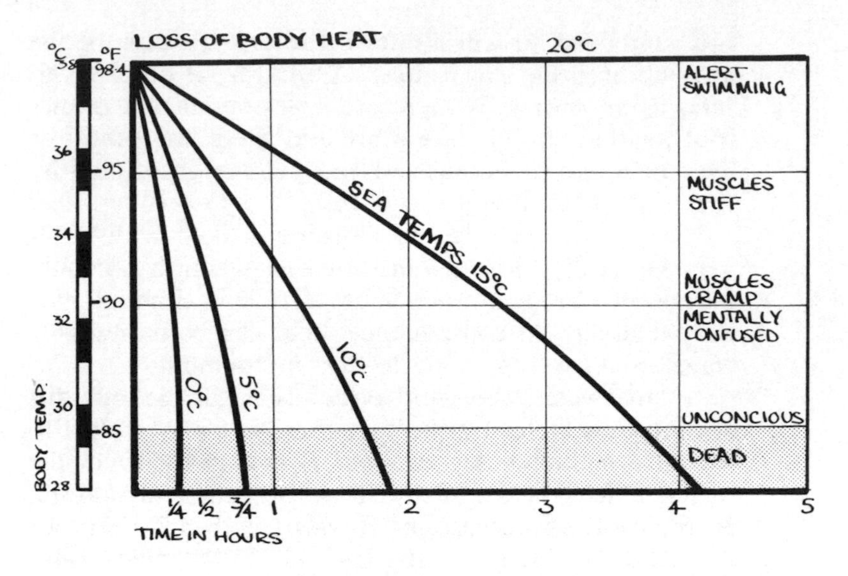

FIG. 35 Loss of body heat

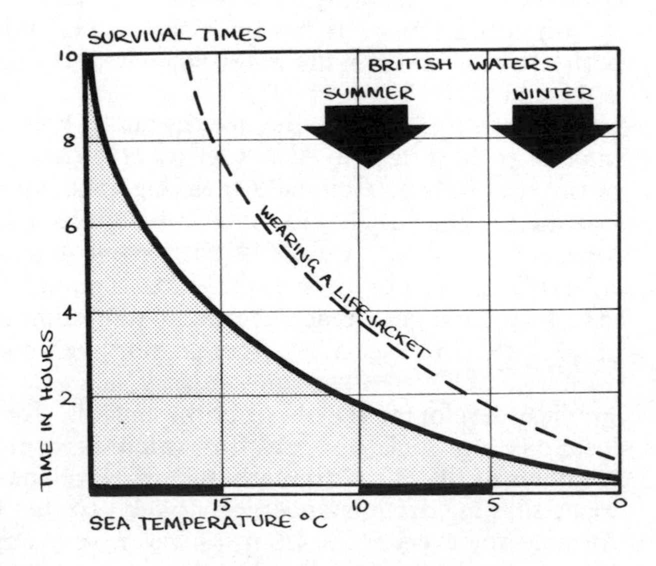

FIG. 36 Survival times

this contained air will diminish the effectiveness of the protection given by clothes. A windproof outer layer, such as an anorak, is therefore an essential part of any foul-weather clothing assembly and there are records of lives being saved because of the protection offered by this type of clothing.

'The insulation value of clothing soaked with water may be as little as one-tenth of that when dry, mainly because water is a much more efficient conductor of heat than air. In consequence, heat can be more easily transferred from the body to the environment.

'In the water, the wind effect is negligible, but this advantage is offset by the fact that heat may be lost to the surrounding water at about *twenty-seven times* the rate at which it is lost in still air at the same temperature. Heavy clothing (especially if worn with a waterproof outer layer) will reduce the loss rate by keeping a layer of water – warmed by the body – close to it.

'This is a principle exploited by the use of the now familiar "wet suit". Clearly this advantage given by clothing, even in water, will be greater if the water contained in the clothing is not being constantly replaced by physical activity. It has been shown that it is much better to remain still in the water when heat conservation is the aim.

'Other factors which influence the rate of body cooling include such factors as age, sex, body build and state of physical fitness. Generally speaking, young fit people fare better than their elders. Women tend to survive longer than men. Certainly fat people have a considerable advantage over thin: indeed moderately fat men may be able to reach thermal equilibrium in water at 15°–18°C (60°–65°F) whereas thin men could not do so.

'The development of hypothermia is frequently insidious and unless a careful watch is kept on all members of the party, the early signs may well be missed, especially as circumstances are likely to be uncomfortable for everybody. It is, however, very important to recognise incipient hypothermia, or exposure, as it is generally called, because death can supervene quite rapidly.

'It is essential to rest the sufferer in a sheltered place, and warm him if disaster is to be avoided.

'Early signs of exposure will be a feeling of coldness, probably associated with shivering, but these two symptoms are quite common and, alone, do not warrant a diagnosis of hypothermia, although they are warning signals. As the condition develops there will be evidence of abnormal behaviour such as listlessness, lack of interest, general slowness, weakness, stumbling and, possibly, numbness of the extremities. When numerous members of a party are dispersed, it may be more difficult to observe these signs.

'Watch should be kept for lack of responsiveness to commands or instructions, failure to maintain station or any other form of irrational behaviour. Later there may be complaint of cramp and possibly nausea and vomiting, vision may be dimmed and the speech slurred. At this time the victim will be very confused and lethargic and make little attempt to help himself. If, at this moment, medical examination were possible, a low blood pressure and a slow, probably irregular pulse would be found, and collapse would be imminent. When collapse occurs, shivering ceases, there is muscle rigidity, respiration is depressed and eventually becomes stertorous. The pupils of the eyes become dilated and, unless treatment is instituted as a matter of urgency, death is inevitable. Because of the depth of the coma, it is sometimes difficult to be sure when death has occurred and it is therefore worth while to attempt resuscitation *in all cases*.

'Treatment of hypothermia involves re-warming the patient as rapidly as possible, and this applies to conscious as well as unconscious patients. If the patient has lost consciousness it is probable that his core temperature has fallen to below 32°C (90°F) and re-warming is urgently necessary. The best way of achieving this is to immerse the patient in a bath of water at 40°C (104°–111°F) – just bearable by the normal elbow – until his general condition is seen to be improving.

'When this has been achieved, he should be removed from the water and allowed to continue his re-warming spontaneously in a warm bed.

'Obviously it is desirable, where possible, to summon medical assistance when treating hypothermic patients. There are other factors, such as blood pressure and cardiac arrhythmias, which may require attention, and there is also the possibility of collapse during treatment. Should a patient's condition deteriorate during re-warming, or should collapse occur, he should be removed from the bath and laid flat with the legs raised to encourage the return of blood to the heart. When he has recovered sufficiently, he may be returned to the bath, but the limbs should, if possible, be elevated. It is, in any case, desirable to keep the limbs out of the water during the re-warming process. If it is found impossible to treat a hypothermic patient by total immersion for any reason (such as repeated collapse or injuries) then immersion of one or two limbs may be effective. Immersion of limbs alone may well be the only way of treating several patients when only one bath is available. In many situations, where no bath is at hand, use must be made of any suitable or available source of heat to achieve re-warming of the patient.

'Should cardiac arrest, with or without cessation of respiration, have occurred either before or during treatment, exhaled air resuscitation (kiss-of-life) must be given immediately and also closed chest cardiac massage. In hypothermic deaths there is evidence to suggest that cardiac arrest occurs before respiratory failure – hence both treatments are often necessary. The techniques are easily mastered, but they must be learnt.

'For the benefit of those familiar with the techniques, the rate at which mouth-to-mouth (and external cardiac massage) are given should be about half the normal rate, because of the low rate of metabolism in the hypothermic body.

'Hypothermia is the most dangerous of conditions caused by exposure to cold, but there are other injuries worthy of mention. Frost-bite, for instance, is due to an actual freezing of body tissue, usually of the extremities, and characteristically, the affected parts look waxy and feel firm on examination. Treatment of this condition again demands re-warming by immersion in water at 40°C (104°F) or by the application of hot fomentations plus pain-relieving drugs which will certainly be required as thawing progresses. Clearly, frost-bite can only occur when flesh is exposed to temperatures below freezing point. Another non-freezing cold injury (sometimes called "immersion foot" or "trench foot") which may affect any part of the body, can be caused by immersion in water at a little above 0°C for several hours, or exposure to cold air for long periods. The affected areas may be very painful, or numb, and may be swollen. Discoloration to a purple or livid hue is usual and the area appears blotchy. It is important to keep the affected limbs dry when treating this condition. The necessary re-warming is achieved by immersing only the patient's trunk in a hot bath, and raising the affected limbs to minimise the swelling which will almost certainly occur.

'From the foregoing discussion it will be apparent that hypothermia is a condition best avoided! Indeed, cold is probably the main threat to life during prolonged immersion in any waters other than tropical ones. It is therefore sensible to assess the risks before sailing on cold water and take all possible precautions to avoid becoming chilled. When the water is very cold, say around 5°C (41°F), a man of ordinary build immersed in it would be hypothermic and helpless in half-an-hour or less. He would be reduced to the same state within one or two hours if the water were 15°C (59°F) although these times may be doubled by the wearing of conventional clothing and even more if special clothing is worn. Some sailing clubs insist on their members wearing "wet-suits" when water temperatures are below 5°C (41°F) and this is a very wise rule because, quite apart from hypothermia, immersion in cold water can cause sudden death, because the shock of immersion makes it difficult to breathe normally.

'Avoiding hypothermia therefore resolves itself into a matter of wearing a sufficiency of warm clothing with a wind-proof and water-proof outer layer. When in the water, it is preferable to float quietly. Wear gloves or mittens whenever possible to minimise the chance of cold injury to the fingers. At sea, a dose of a sea-sickness remedy, such as hyoscine, will help to prevent a malady which adds to one's heat losses, as well as sapping all-important morale. Such simple measures save lives. Often the cause of death in victims of accidents in the water has been assumed to be "drowning" whereas it is now thought probable that hypothermia was the principal cause of death, and drowning was merely a terminal event.

'There seems to exist a considerable ignorance about the dangers of immersion in cold water, or alternatively, there is a reluctance to accept that the hazard is important. Measures are taken to avoid ordinary physical injury and drowning and, indeed, most sportsmen and others are familiar with the first aid treatment of these conditions.

'More and more enthusiastic sailors, canoeists and others use their boats all the year round, even when conditions are extremely cold. In general, such activity should be encouraged, but with reservations, because there is no doubt that there is an appreciable hazard, although the risks can be reduced to an acceptable level by sensible appreciation of the simple actions necessary to reduce the possibility of injury by cold.'

CHAPTER FOUR

Emergency Situations Afloat

The worst thing that can happen when you are sailing is to fall out and lose contact with the boat. The lesser evil is to capsize the boat and find yourself swimming with it. Since the publication of the RYA Training Method, considerable discussion has taken place regarding the advisability of teaching novice sailors to sail in boats which can be capsized, and a well-known journalist has used it as a regular item for his editorial on the basis that it is unreasonable to teach a skill which would not be needed if boats didn't capsize. Our view remains unchanged – it is because the majority of sailing dinghies can capsize, even in skilled hands, that we continue to train novices in self-rescue skills so that they will be self reliant and not have to call upon the rescue services except in case of genuine emergency.

THE 'SCOOP' RIGHTING SEQUENCE

There are several ways of righting a capsized dinghy – this is a proven economical sequence offering a high success rate without the need to swim the boat around to suit the wind direction. There are many factors which dictate what should be done in the event of a capsize. Whatever else happens, contact with the boat must be maintained, so that, should the need for eventual rescue arise, the crew will be with the most identifiable object, the hull of the upturned boat (Fig. 37). For our purposes, we shall consider a capsize in moderate wind and wave conditions, such that a practical routine will result in a successful righting. The object of the righting sequence in a training programme is to ensure that beginners will accept a capsize as an integral part of dinghy sailing. It is as well to remember that boats were designed to be sailed, and a capsize is a potentially dangerous situation, especially so when the practice of sitting on the side of the

FIG. 37 Stay with the boat

boat, to keep dry, results in an inversion over the unfortunate crew.

This detailed sequence does away with the need for immediate lowering of sails and unnecessary positioning of the boat by swimming. In its entirety, it provides the novice with a logical progression of actions designed to get the boat upright and sailing in the shortest possible time. In a modified form it can be used by the racing helmsman to continue sailing within a minute of capsize.

In the sequence, the helmsman and crew have specific tasks. In the event of the crew being much heavier than the helmsman their roles should be reversed. We have assumed that the mainsail is transom-sheeted.

Fig. 38a: When the boat capsizes the helmsman and crew fall into the water on the same side as the sail. After checking that both are free of the sails, they make their way back to the transom, retaining contact with the boat. Helmsman checks that the rudder is secure. Crew frees the mainsheet and passes the end to the helmsman to use as a safety line.

Fig. 38b: If the centreboard is not down, the helmsman steadies the boat with the rudder whilst the crew swims back and pulls the board down. Helmsman swims to centreboard watched by the crew. Helmsman steadies the boat by holding the centreboard or placing his arms over it. The crew moves from the transom to the inside.

Fig. 38c: The crew throws a jib sheet to the helmsman, who acknowledges its receipt. The crew then lies down in the

FIG. 38A-F Righting after capsize using the 'scoop' righting sequence

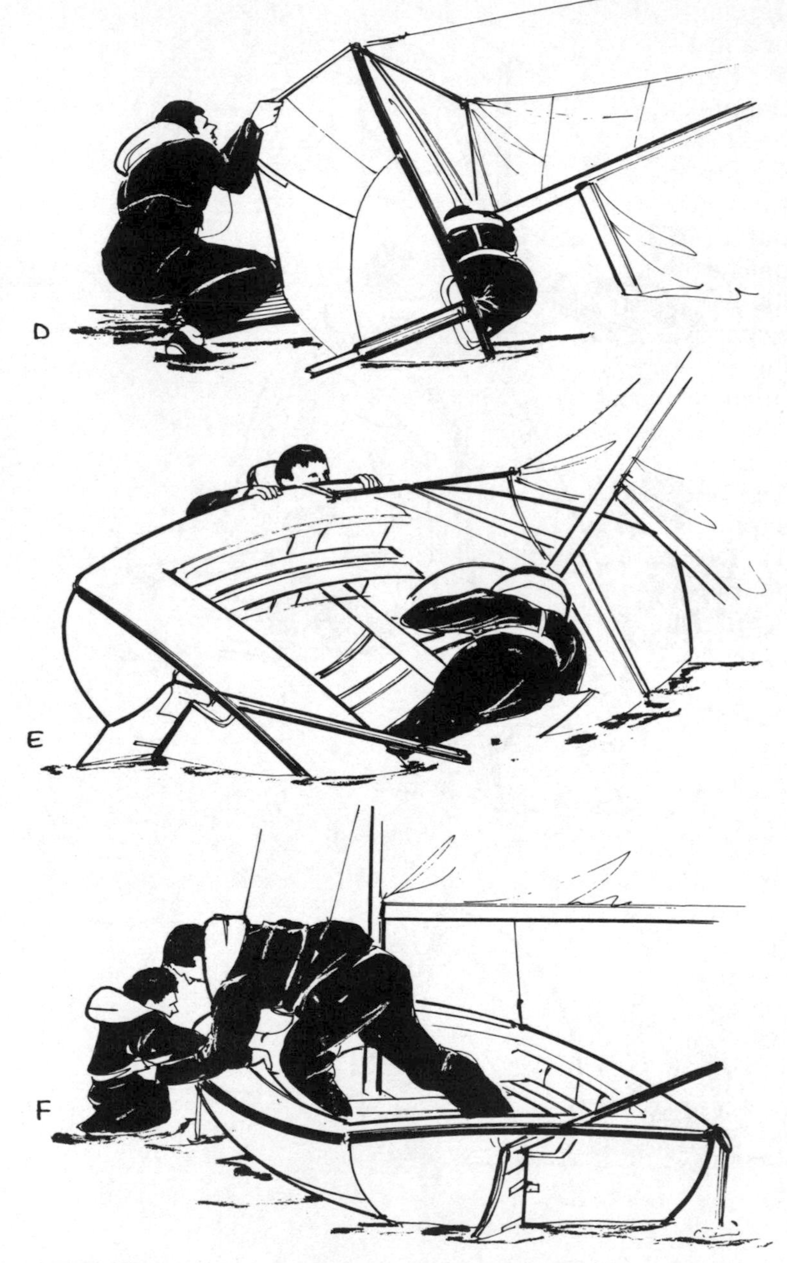

FIG. 38 cont.

boat supported by the water and facing forward, knees on the inside of the gunwale.

Note: In boats which have large side tanks and which float very high, it may be necessary to climb into the boat and rock it towards the helmsman to initiate the righting.

Fig. 38d–e/ The crew tells the helmsman when he is ready. The helmsman uses the jib sheet to climb up on the centreboard as near the root of the board as possible then leans back pulling on the jib sheet until the boat 'unsticks' and comes slowly upright, scooping up the crew.

Fig. 38f: When the boat is upright the crew waits for the boom to swing over his head (windward capsize) and scrambles to his feet to help the helmsman aboard. The helmsman may climb aboard unaided or the crew may have to rock the boat towards the helmsman so that the side is immersed and he slides in with the water. The helmsman sails the boat on a reach, helping the crew to bail out the surplus water.

Centre Mainsheets

Crews who sail racing dinghies equipped with centre mainsheets are usually skilful at recovering their boats from a knockdown position, but when crew or helmsman fall in the following sequence will guarantee that they will get the boat upright at the first attempt even in a capsize to windward.

Whoever is nearest the centreboard goes to it, the other crew member throws a jib sheet over and positions himself aft of the mainsheet (Fig. 39) holding on to the lower toe straps. As the boat is pulled upright the side of the boat contacts

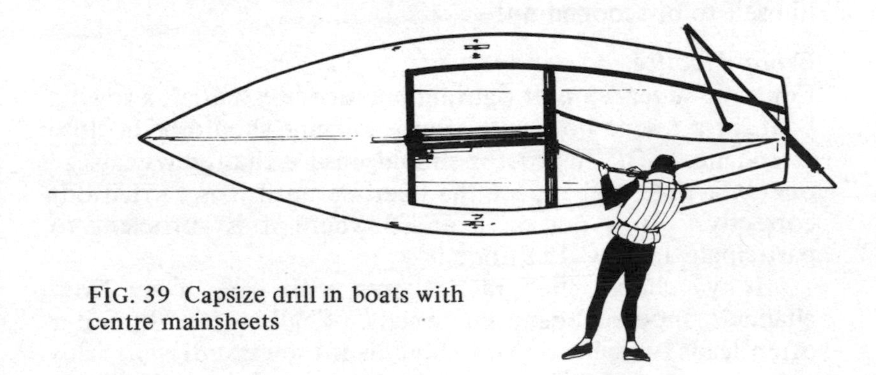

FIG. 39 Capsize drill in boats with centre mainsheets

the crew's lower chest area and scoops him into the boat, or in a windward capsize allows him to stay dangling over the side to counterbalance the capsizing force of the mainsail. Helmsman and crew scramble aboard together.

Single-handed Boats

With the increased use of one-man boats Instructors must give advice on their righting. Some boats can be righted by applying weight to the centreboard, but the absence of jib sheets makes this a strenuous task. Skilled single-handers favour the knockdown where the boat is permitted to be knocked flat whilst they climb over the side to stand on the daggerboard and pull the boat upright.

An alternative method, particularly with an inverted boat, is to right it from the bow by applying weight so that the bow is immersed and the stern and rear half of the boat rears clear of the water, and then rotate the hull until it rights, and get aboard by sliding along the windward side until the cockpit is reached, grab the toe straps and haul yourself aboard.

Riding the Board

The extremely skilled single-hander, or two-man sailor faced with a windward capsize, will apply weight gently to the centreboard until the wind gets under the mainsail, then slide quickly over and duck down under the board so that he is now wrapped around the board and being pressed into it as the boat rights. As he comes up the other side, still wrapped around the board, his weight will prevent the boat capsizing.

In a crewed boat the other crew member should position himself to be scooped up!

Group Practice

Constant supervision of righting practice is essential; a rowing boat, or a rescue boat with stopped engine should be in close attendance. The Instructor should ensure that crews capsize one at a time and repeat the exercise until it is carried out correctly. It is not an exercise where it is sufficient to participate and say 'I've done it'.

Always choose the practice area with care, away from channels, moored boats and weeds. Shallow muddy water often leads to jammed main halyards if the mast digs in. This can be prevented by securing an old lifejacket to the mast; it may also be advisable to keep an old suit of sails for practice work.

The best time to carry out the practice is at the end of a session or a day's sailing so that pupils may change their clothing afterwards.

It will be necessary to arrange a land session beforehand to detail the method and familiarise pupils with both roles, as each will right the boat as helmsman and crew.

Righting a boat can be hard work, therefore we recommend the following procedures to be followed, in the event of failure to right the boat.

After one attempt the crew should inflate their lifejackets. After the second attempt the mainsail is lowered by releasing the main halyard. Care should be taken to lash the sail and the boom to the boat, to prevent it sinking. When all is reasonably under control, the righting sequence should be carried out.

Failure at the third attempt indicates that the crew are unlikely to right the boat unaided. They should therefore secure themselves to the boat and await rescue (Fig. 37). Obviously the above advice applies only to a controlled teaching situation. A lone boat, capsized four miles off a rocky headland, or being swept along a deserted beach, will be in a completely different situation. In the first instance, ensure that there is no possibility of either crew or helmsman being parted from the boat. A successful righting should be followed by an immediate reduction in sail area to cope with the conditions. The most essential thing is to stop trying to right the boat before the crew become too exhausted to secure themselves to it, and thereafter attract attention. This advice must be coupled with the sections of this book which deal with hypothermia. If a crew have practised righting their boat many times, they stand a much greater chance of not getting into dangerous situations.

Novices should be given advice concerning action in the event of a dinghy capsizing on top of them. There is a lot of room under a modern boat, therefore they will not suffer from lack of air (Fig. 40). There is also plenty of light reflected from the surrounding water; in fact, an upturned boat

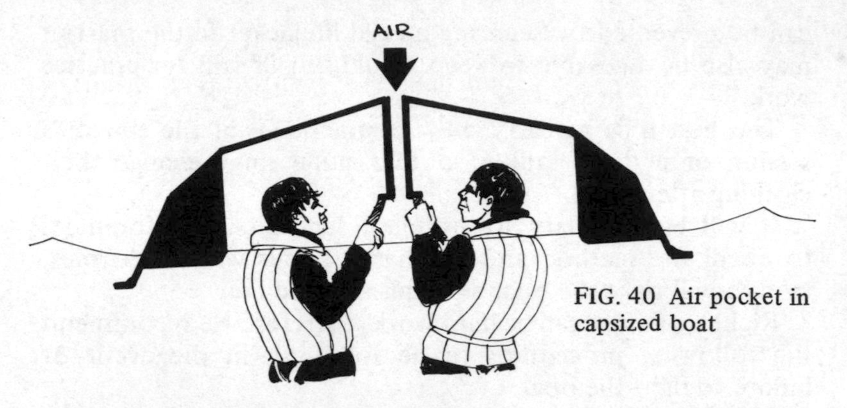

FIG. 40 Air pocket in capsized boat

offers peace and protection! Novices are often reluctant to attempt to extricate themselves because of their unfamiliarity with boats, therefore an Instructor should go down with them to bring them out. This is one instance when an Instructor makes his own decision about wearing a lifejacket and the exact method of helping the pupils out. He can either ensure that lifejackets are deflated and then duck down under the gunwale with each pupil, or remove their lifejackets, getting the pupils to push them out in front of them until they are on the outside. The latter method may be necessary if pupils are worried about getting caught on the gunwale as they duck down. In cases of panic or claustrophobia, right the boat with outside help.

Righting an Inverted Boat

Unaided. An inverted boat presents a number of problems to the crew. The mast may stick in the mud preventing any further action or the centreboard may fall back into the case, or worse, out of the boat.

Assuming that neither of these mishaps occurs, the crew should set about sinking one of the 'corners' (Fig. 41) of the boat. Two-man crews normally sink a quarter. The single-handed sailor often uses the bow so that when the boat rights it is head to wind.

When the boat resumes a normal capsized position the crew should set about righting in the usual way.

Aided. Safety and rescue boats often cause considerable

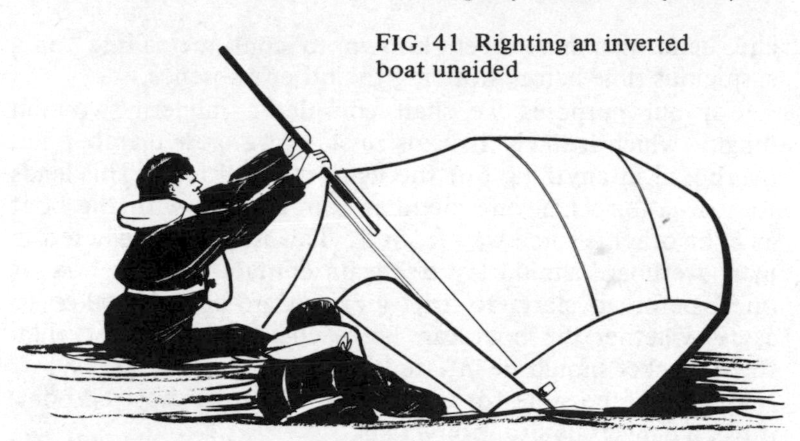

FIG. 41 Righting an inverted boat unaided

damage when attempting this righting manoeuvre, and heavy launches are not ideal. The rescue boat noses its bow into the area forward of the shrouds while the dinghy's crew position themselves on the opposite side using their weight to sink it. The safety-boat crew grasp the shroud or trapeze wire and work their way hand over hand towards the mast-head, pulling the boat up as they go.

The safety boat is kept in position by oars, not the engine. By the time the dinghy is on its side the safety boat will be clear of the forestay and jib and can support the mast until the crew are ready to start the righting sequence. Whatever happens, the mainsail should not be unshackled at the mast-head, otherwise when the boat is righted the main halyard will be at the top of the mast and the only way of getting it down will be to capsize the boat!

MAN OVERBOARD

Many generations of sailors and fishermen have gone to sea without being able to swim. It is only recently, with the introduction of lightweight sailing dinghies, that we have considered that it is advisable to be able to swim. The sailors and fishermen knew that to fall overboard from a large sailing ship would be fatal and that their ability to swim would only prolong the agony. They also knew that many masters were working to tight time-schedules and would not spare the time to round up to pick up a lost crew member. Man overboard in a dinghy is quite a different thing – though some crews and helmsmen have been known to continue sailing for a suspicious time before noticing the other's absence.

For our purposes we shall consider a modern two-man dinghy which is likely to capsize should a crew member fall overboard in anything but the lightest conditions. This leads to a situation when one member is in contact with the boat and the other is some way from it. This is one case where the man overboard should try to regain contact with the boat at once, before it starts to drift away. Care must be taken to assess whether the boat can be reached. If it cannot, then the lifejacket should be inflated immediately.

It may be possible for the crew to right the capsized boat; if not a dangerous situation exists.

There is not a simple solution to this situation. For instance, to anchor the boat to prevent it drifting away is sound advice *only* in non-tidal conditions, or where the boat is downwind of the isolated crew. Neither can one assume that the boat and the isolated crew will drift in the same direction. An onshore wind will certainly take the wind-borne boat and occupant to the beach, but the west-going tidal stream will take the tide-borne isolated crew along the coast (Fig. 42). When searching for lost crews carefully ascertain the exact point of man overboard and plot the

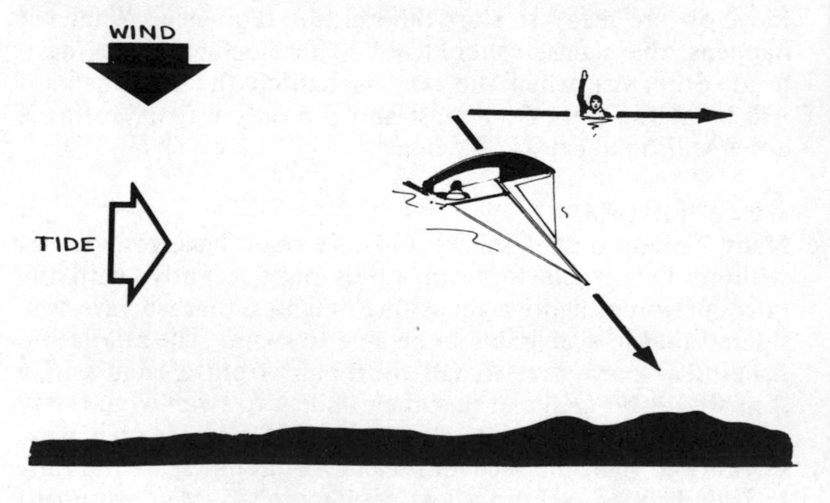

FIG. 42 Boat is wind-borne, crew is tide-borne

movement of both from that point, taking into consideration wind and tidal changes.

Where the boat remains upright a completely different situation exists. For many years novices have been taught a man overboard recovery method which is unsound. It is based on the unlikely premise that the crew is overboard and the helmsman is able to gybe the boat and pick him up. In practice it is never as simple as this. The helmsman often falls overboard which leaves a crew to carry out the gybe. If it was blowing hard enough for both to be sitting out, then the gybe will be difficult, especially so as the two-man boat will now be grossly over-canvassed – or under-crewed. Such a situation will inevitably result in the boat capsizing during the gybe, thus leaving the man overboard in an extremely dangerous situation.

Novices should be taught a method which relates to their early sailing and which allows them sufficient time to regain control of themselves and the boat without losing track of the man in the water. Their subsequent actions should be such that the boat stands a reasonable chance of remaining upright to effect the rescue.

Man Overboard Recovery

1. A crew member falls overboard. He inflates his lifejacket and keeps his eyes on the boat. One hand is raised vertically.
2. The remaining crew gains control of the boat, adjusts the sails and marking the position of the man in the water, sails on to a beam reach centreboard fully *down*.
3. When he is sufficient distance away, fifty to seventy-five metres, the 'helmsman' marks the man in the water and goes about from a reach to a reach sailing back towards the man in the water.
4. With just sufficient drive to move the boat at a moderate approach speed, the helmsman steers a broad reach to a point where he can round up on to a close-hauled course and sail directly to the man in the water. (Fig. 43.)
5. As the boat rounds up and stops adjacent to the man in the water the helmsman moves forward on the windward side pulling the tiller to windward as the boat stops.

6. Standing behind the windward shroud the helmsman grasps the man overboard and pauses while the boat assumes a hove-to position (Fig. 44). The crew climbs aboard.

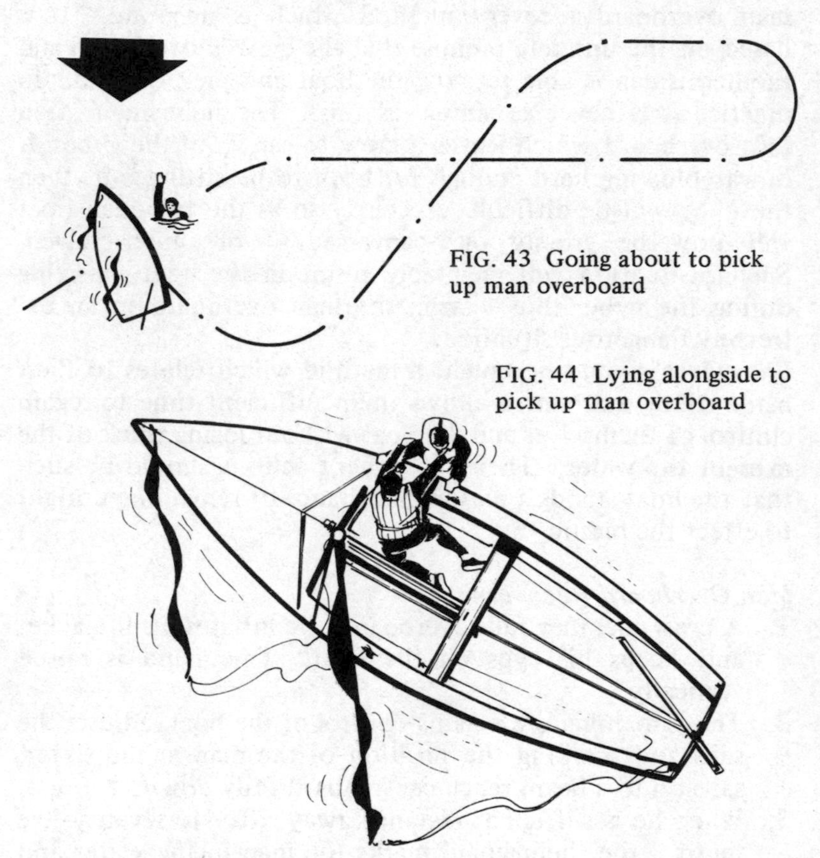

FIG. 43 Going about to pick up man overboard

FIG. 44 Lying alongside to pick up man overboard

Hauling aboard often presents problems. It sometimes helps to rock the boat so that the gunwale is immersed as the man overboard is pulled in. Hauling in over the transom is not recommended. The boat automatically bears away and begins to sail off out of control. In addition the tiller is easily damaged, and worse still, it is not pleasant to be dragged over a sharp-edged, gadget-cluttered transom.

In circumstances other than a controlled teaching situation, it may be necessary to lash the man overboard alongside and make for the shore – taking care not to tack. If the boat is off-shore with no hope of outside assistance, it may be necessary to capsize the boat to windward if all else fails, and carry out a normal righting procedure. This must be regarded as an extreme measure for an extreme situation.

Getting a man back onboard is difficult, especially if he is exhausted or injured. Sails may be used as strops or mainsheet tackles may be utilised. Whatever method is used it is easier to haul aboard one part of the body at a time taking care to secure it, rather than try to lift the whole body.

Man Overboard Practice

It is not necessary to insist on an actual man overboard situation as in the righting sequence. However, it is not sufficient to throw a bottle or lifejacket overboard and then recover it. Fig. 45 shows a suggested simulated man-overboard dummy made up of perforated polythene cans and bottles, dressed in clothes and supported by an old lifejacket. The object of the exercise is not only for pupils to practise the correct sequence

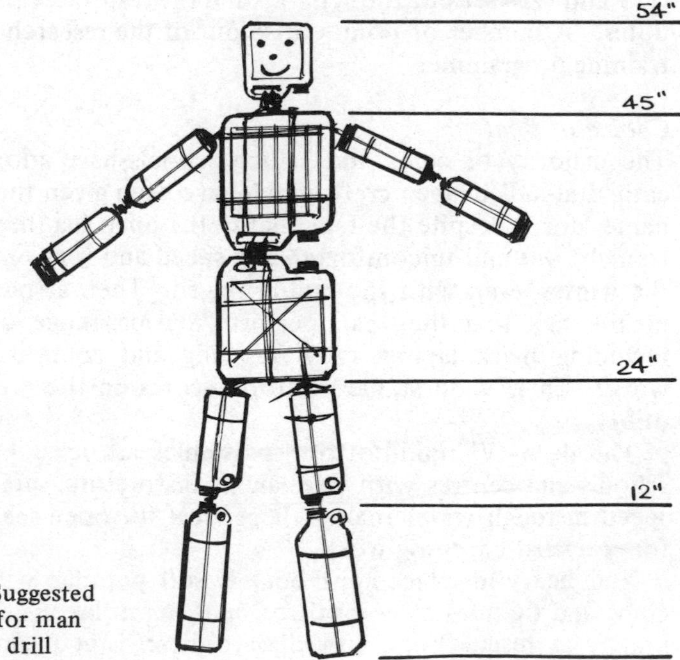

FIG. 45 Suggested 'dummy' for man overboard drill

of events to bring them back to the victim but also to give them practical experience, as helmsmen, in recovering the victim. The polythene-can dummy, filled with water, presents sufficient problems for the pupils to appreciate the difficulties of getting a body back on board.

SAFETY BOATS AND RESCUE CRAFT

Rescue craft are those boats used for saving life. Safety boats are salvage craft and those engaged in supervisory duties. If only one craft is used and has to combine the functions it must be fast enough to carry out the prime duty of a rescue craft and save lives.

The National Sportsboat Certificate

The RYA has recently introduced a new training scheme to cater for the needs of drivers of sportsboats and runabouts, and a more advanced award – the Rescue Boat Coxswain's Endorsement. The latter qualification is intended to train rescue boat crews to a national standard. RYA publications G19 and G20 set out the syllabus and the respective Instructor notes. A number of points arise out of the research into the training programme.

Choice of Boat

The majority of clubs and sailing schools have adopted the cathedral-hulled open craft which have been given the generic name 'dory', despite the fact that in the open sea they are extremely wet and uncomfortable at speed and very exposed in the winter, even with the cuddy rigged. Their attraction lies in the fact that they can perform a wide range of duties including mark laying, crew ferrying and committee boat work. Their wide stable platform scores on the grounds of utility.

The deep 'V' rigid-bottom inflatables are used by sailing schools and centres with permanent Instructors; their greater speed in rough water makes them ideal for open-sea use and for specialist coaching work.

The heavy displacement boat is still popular with many clubs and doubles as committee boat, mark layer and occasionally as rescue boat. Its inboard diesel is economical and reliable and it can usually be driven by a variety of skippers without too much wear and tear.

Equipment

Small fast boats can carry a limited range of safety equipment. They should have their own anchor and chain stowed in such a way that the coxswain can drop the anchor over the side and the boat will moor itself; also one or two smaller anchors which can be used to secure drifting boats until they can be recovered.

Perhaps the most useful piece of equipment is an orange marker buoy attached to fifty metres of plaited rope. It can be used as a tow rope floated down on to a capsized craft, or as a rescue line for a boat aground on a lee shore, or as a marker buoy for sailing exercises. When not in use it can be stowed ready for immediate use in a large industrial bucket which itself can be used for a wide variety of purposes!

Flares and smoke flares must be carried when operating in open-sea conditions to draw attention to an emergency situation. Alternative means of propulsion should be provided, usually oars but sometimes a smaller outboard motor.

Safety boats with their larger hulls and extended duties as supervisory craft should be comprehensively fitted out to provide mobile first aid facilities including substantial shelter and cooking facilities for the provision of hot drinks. For salvaging abandoned dinghies, a heavy displacement boat should work in conjunction with rescue craft, especially in rough seas, to ensure that the salvaged craft is not damaged further.

CHAPTER FIVE

Race Training and Organisation

After the introduction of the National Proficiency and Coaching Scheme, it became obvious that the next development programme would centre around race training. I am indebted to Alastair Mitchell and Eric Triname for experimenting with the schedules which eventually formed the basis for the introduction of the National Youth Racing Scheme as a first step to a totally comprehensive scheme of race training for club sailors.

Britain is still ranked as one of the top sailing nations but our successes are increasingly centred around the offshore classes. Our dinghy sailors continue to win world titles but since the last Olympics it has become increasingly difficult to do so, and our crews need to train constantly ashore and afloat. This is no surprise because in my capacity as Secretary to the IYRU Youth Committee in the early seventies, I was able to observe the importance such countries as Spain, Holland, Israel and the United States placed on the success of their youth crews. Whether those countries' programmes benefit a wide range of sailing talent or just a small elite is debatable but in the harsh spotlight of top-flight competition countries tend to be judged by their success.

The training programmes devised for the youth racing scheme are broadly based on young club sailors, embodying a ladder system of progression and talent spotting which will enable young sailors to first sail in regional squads, then national squads where they will receive regular coaching. Selection for the British Team for the World Youth Championship will remain in the form of sailing trials to ensure that every young sailor has the opportunity to compete.

So much for the state of British racing. This chapter is primarily concerned with the novice who has just learned to sail and wishes to learn something about racing, or the newcomer to the club who has been equipped with his membership badge, key and tie but who does not quite understand the complicated fixture list which sets out the multitude of class races, handicap events and special events which threaten to take up every minute of his spare time – once he has learned to race!

Basic Race Training Programme
The first race training programme is designed to teach the basic concepts of racing covering such topics as how races are organised, started, sailed and finished, and the simplest sailing rules as applied to the racing situation.

Sessions afloat are designed to increase basic boat-handling skills including a follow-my-leader session around a triangular course to ensure that everyone knows where they should sail. Thereafter sessions are spent practising starts, mark rounding and finishing using a variety of short courses.

The aim of a basic race training course is to ensure that when the participants enter their first race they have some idea of what to expect and what is expected of them. Subsequent race training courses differ only in their degree of difficulty and the standard expected from the participants.

Racing Equipment
Thc trainer needs to be self sufficient with a supply of buoys sufficient to lay a triangular course for racing or a slalom course for practising upwind tacking, downwind gybing. Six is a minimum.
A whistle is the simplest sound signal.
A number board to signify times or boat numbers.
Flag signals to advise the fleet of specific manoeuvres – marks to port or starboard – or go home!
A recording pad.
A chart and compass to set the courses.
Most race training is carried out from a boat, entailing proper stowage facilities for equipment.

Training Courses
A basic triangular course with a wing mark to port can be modified to a letter E course by the addition of two buoys.

A slalom course is quite simple to set especially if a wire trace is used and the slalom line is anchored at one end only so that it is wind rode.

The square course offers a wide variety of possibilities especially when an additional mark is laid at its centre. Two starting lines of about 200 yards length are laid 200 yards apart (Fig. 46). Starting and finishing using long lines teaches position planning and permits upwind and downwind starts and a rapid turn round with numerous 'races'.

The addition of a buoy in the centre of the course transforms the situation permitting the variations shown in Fig. 47.

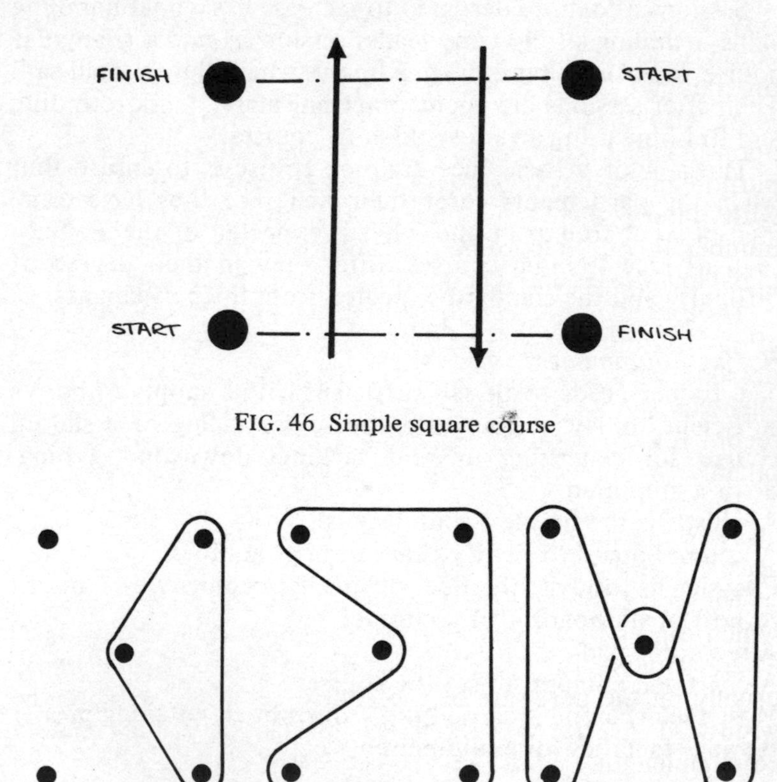

FIG. 46 Simple square course

FIG. 47 Variations based on a square course

Starting Intervals

The most striking change from normal racing is the time interval for the starting sequence. Five-minute intervals are a luxury we cannot afford so it is reduced to a minute as follows: 2 minute signal, 1 minute signal, start.

Subsequent classes start on each subsequent minute. The time should be displayed on a board which is shown as the whistle is blown and dropped at the start.

Group Organisation

Groups should be arranged according to ability. Experienced racing crews should not be included with novices. They will very soon feel the need to demonstrate their often incorrect 'knowledge', thus disrupting even the most carefully planned programme!

As with the basic teaching method, initial work is based upon practical sessions afloat. It will be necessary to have a purpose-made racing kit comprising a movable starting line, with intermediate markers, starting flags with flagstaff, number boards, recording instruments, course marks, binoculars, loud hailer and a code of signals to direct the group.

Thorough briefing ashore will avoid hours of wasted time afloat. Groups of six boats form a good working unit. If possible, each group should have a distinguishing colour and all boats should be numbered on each bow, if an accurate record is to be kept, or if photographs or recordings are being taken.

The practice area should be chosen with care, preferably away from shipping channels, strong tides or crowded anchorages.

The course should be compact, comprising a starting line which can easily be changed from a port to a starboard bias. There should also be a windward mark and a wing mark, usually on the port side of the course, set at 60°–90° to the windward mark. All three legs should be approximately equal in length.

The Rules of the Road

Before going afloat, it is essential that all participating crews understand the basic rules for the prevention of collisions at sea. In particular, the rules governing port- and starboard-tack racing dinghies must be explained. It sometimes helps crews to remember their rights of way, if green tape is placed on the port side. Red for 'danger', green for 'go'. In the initial stages, crews should not be tempted to 'stand on their rights', and should always turn away if a collision seems likely.

Points of greatest contact occur at the start and finish, and at marks when they are being rounded. As each is a special case, each should be the subject of special sessions ashore and afloat.

Race training is intended to promote competent boat handling, sound understanding of the racing rules, and a sense of sportsmanship allied to the desire to win.

Boat Handling in Groups

An introductory session afloat is used to ensure that the crews

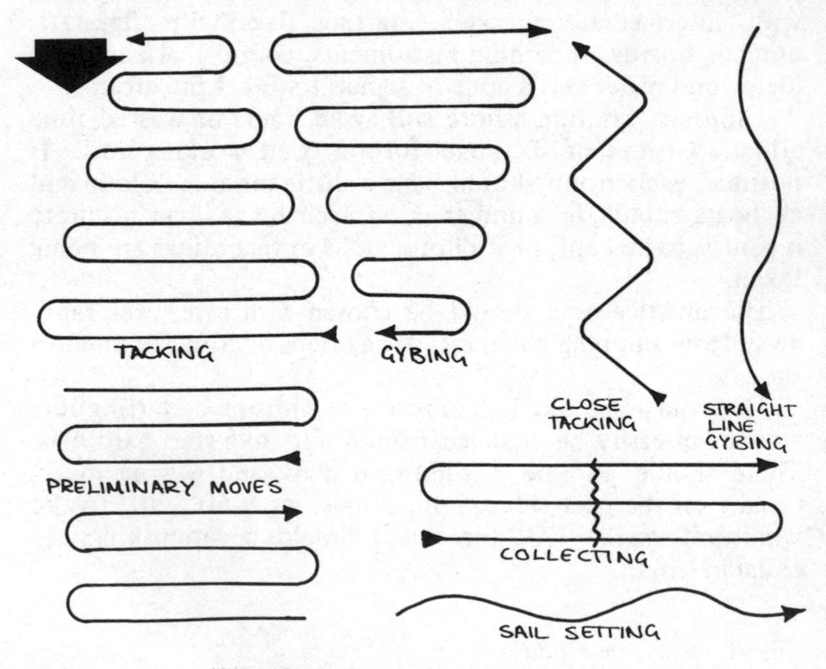

FIG. 48 'Follow my leader' exercises

have an opportunity to handle their boats in close company. The Instructor should lead the group into the 'follow-my-leader' exercises which begin as simple 'snaking' manoeuvres and progress to short, and gybing, exercises with the boats only a few feet apart. Fig. 48 shows a suggested pattern to be followed. Care must be taken to avoid a situation which requires that boats should cross each other at an angle, as sometimes seen at motor-cycle displays! After each set of turns, the group should be made to sail on a straight course, until stragglers have re-formed. Each boat should aim to turn on the same spot as the lead boat. Early or late turns cause confusion.

Distances are expressed as units of the total length of the string of dinghies. Boats which overrun should, when on the wind, luff to windward, slow down and rejoin the string, and when sailing downwind, should haul in their sails and lower their centreboards to slow the boat. Boats which fail to rejoin should go to the back, the remainder should bunch up.

The lead boat should vary the speed to test the crews thoroughly. Skipper changes should take place after each sequence.

'Following-leader' exercises are also used after novices have completed their first solo, and for the teaching of spinnaker and strong wind sailing. The interval between the boats should then be increased to four or five boat lengths.

Starts and Finishes

The Start. Without doubt, the easiest way to lose a race is to start after the rest of the fleet. It is, therefore, essential, in a training programme, to teach novices this aspect of racing, as a separate entity.

Racing helmsmen always try to start a race with clear wind and clear water. There are two ways of achieving this ideal: the first is to make a perfect start, and the second is to wait until everybody else has gone!

Perfect starts are normally the preserve of experienced racing crews who, despite the efforts of their competitors, invariably manage to choose their starting position. Their experience of starting enables them to plan ahead, their actions are deliberate, and they have contingency plans to deal with competitors' obstructive tactics. If we accept that experience of starting leads to more competent starts, it follows that starting practice will be a valuable exercise for all racing crews. However, in a normal racing season, the average club member will have only twenty or thirty starts and it will take very many years to build up the necessary starting experience.

Efficient Control. As with any group activity, success is dependent upon efficient organisation. It has been found that a dummy run, before starting the twelve start series, gives the crews a chance to get their bearings. The purpose of each session must be clearly understood by each crew member.

If the session happens to be on 'Starting' then the remainder of the race is incidental and the finishing position recorded only for the Instructor's benefit. This should be made clear to the pupils.

The Starting Line Angle. Another object of race training is to present helmsmen with situations and circumstances which will encourage them to become more proficient. From the simple start, set with a starboard bias, two simple truths will emerge. Starboard-tack boats have the advantage of position and right-of-way. The right-hand sector of the line gives the boat clear wind and the opportunity to dictate tactics.

A line set square to the wind will still favour those boats which are on starboard tack. In this case boats will normally 'feed in' to the starboard end of the line and range down the line on starboard tack, waiting for the starting signal. This leaves a gap at either end of the line. Those boats coming in to the port end of the line, on port tack, can only hope to tack under the lee of the leading starboard-tack boat, and, thereafter, secure a good position.

A Port Bias Line. If the line is changed so that the port end is moved towards the wind, assuming a windward first leg, it will be seen that there comes a point when a port-tack boat can just cross a starboard-tack boat (Fig. 49). An oft-quoted angle is five degrees of port bias. In the training situation it can be made more, to exaggerate the advantage. Once again,

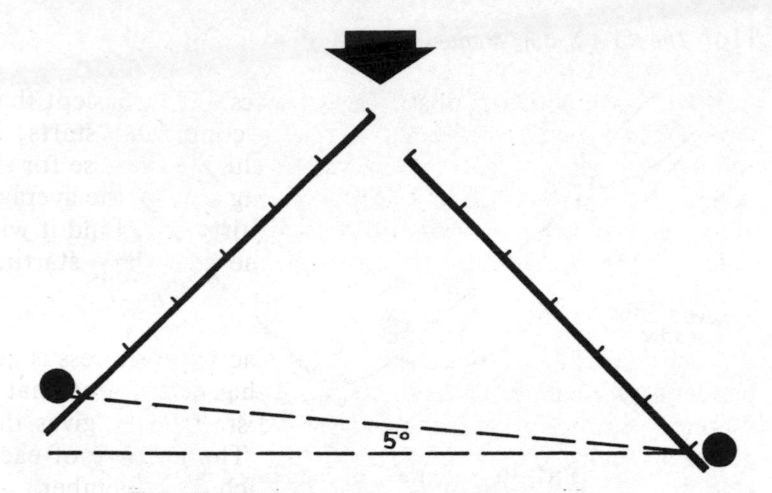

FIG. 49 The advantage of a port-biased line

boats which start on the signal have the advantage, but this time those on port-tack have a chance to get clear wind and to dictate tactics.

Successful port-tack starts, which clear the fleet, require courage. Usually, a good port-tack start can place the boat in a position where it can tack near a starboard-tack boat in a safe position (known as the lee-bow position). Thereafter it can keep in contact with the leaders.

A boat will either point up into the wind, and sail slowly, or it can sail five degrees off close-hauled and sail quickly. At the start it is important to sail quickly and establish a good leading position. Proximity to other competitors at this stage can only serve to slow a boat down. Fortunately the starting exercises encourage crews to drive their boats for the starting line early in the practice sessions. They become accustomed to the idea that boat speed is more important than pointing ability.

Rounding Marks. Since the introduction of the racing rule which permits offending boats to re-round the mark which has been hit, many crews have tended to allow their boats to come much closer to marks. Fig. 50 shows two ways of rounding a mark. The dotted line shows how it *should* be done – a planned wide approach, enabling helmsman and crew to trim their sails during the turn so that the boat is travelling at its maximum speed.

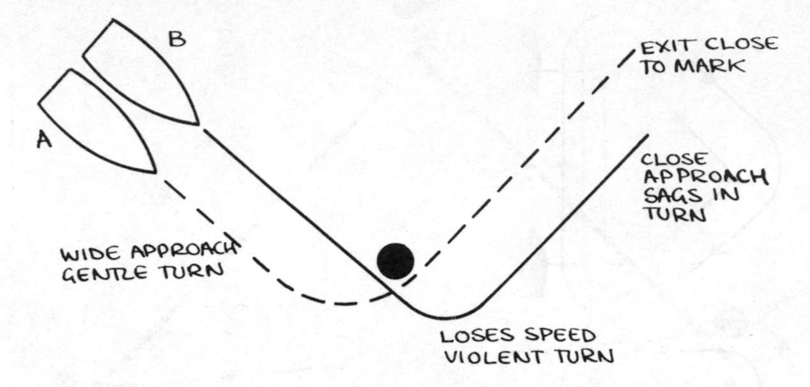

FIG. 50 Two ways of rounding a mark

The boat is only close to the buoy at the end of the rounding, on course for the next mark. This basic technique applies to all forms of rounding. However, also in Fig. 50, it will be seen that the course indicated by the solid line necessitates a close approach followed by a sharp slowing turn, after the buoy is cleared. Such a rounding can only lose speed and position. In a racing situation the proximity of other boats must be taken into consideration but, in the situation indicated, boat 'A' could well squeeze inside boat 'B' and gain the advantage. The key to rounding marks properly is practice, hours and hours of it. Such practice leads to a complete understanding of each type of rounding and to competent boat handling and precise control.

The Instructor should arrange a set sequence for pupils to practise rounding marks. Such organisation will not waste time afloat. It is usually wise to lay marks, rather than to use a trot of moorings. Owners of boats do not welcome strings of cavorting dinghies! Two or three boats may work together, provided there are sufficient markers. Fig. 51 shows a selection of race training exercises. It is possible to allow three boats to work together using four marks, provided they work in unison. Preliminary exercises should be confined to three or four roundings. Tacking on to, and gybing round, buoys is included in the later sequences, to co-ordinate crew responses.

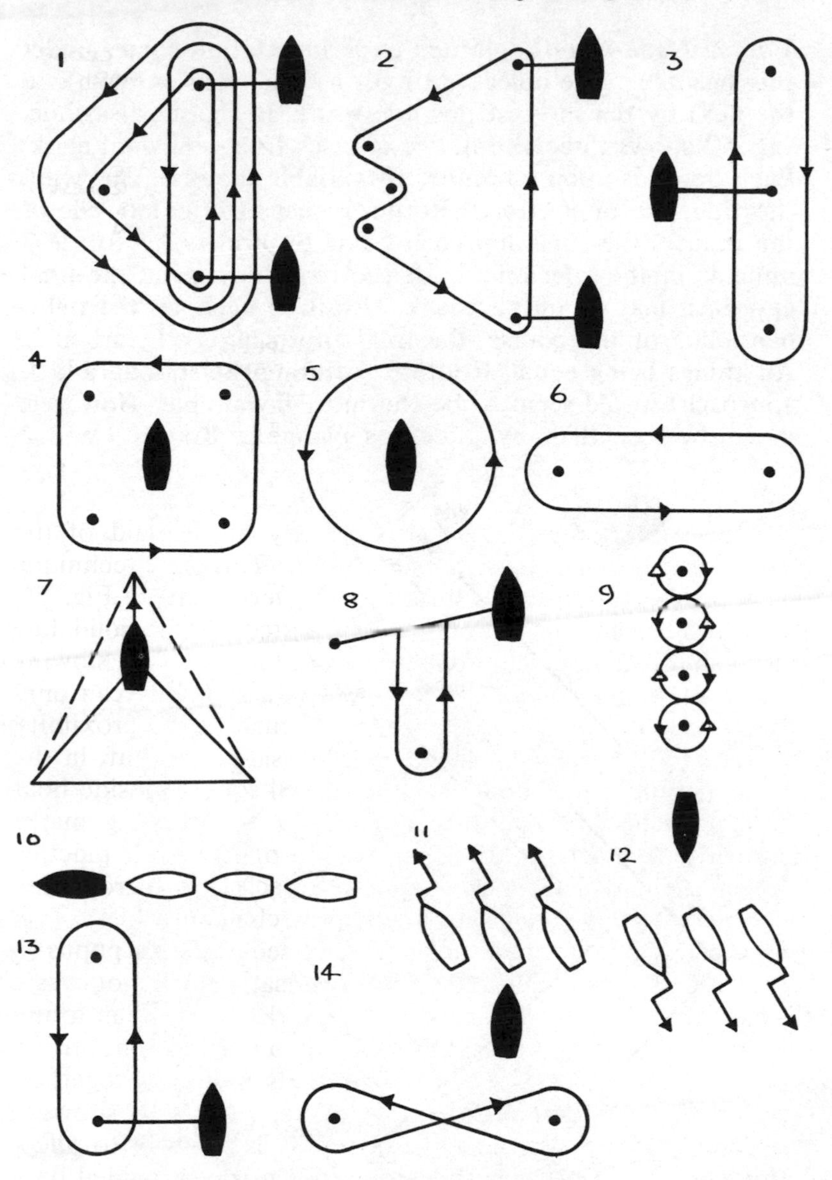

FIG. 51 Selection of race training exercises. Sound signals: one short blast–turn 90° to starboard; two short blasts–turn 90° to port; one long blast–hoist/lower spinnaker; series of short blasts–scatter!

'Course Made Good'. Much experimentation comes under this heading. The object is to get a boat from one mark to the next by the shortest possible route, in the shortest time. Fig. 52 shows three alternative courses to a windward mark. Each depends upon a number of variable factors. The wind, the tide, the opposition. Route 1 keeps to the left side of the course, the final approach being on port-tack. Route 2 remains in the safer middle of the road but, again, the final approach may be on port-tack. Route 3 occupies the right-hand side of the course, the final approach is on starboard. All things being equal, Route 3 (offering the starboard-tack approach) would seem to be the most favourable. However, it can be seen that, by judicious planning, Routes 1 and 2

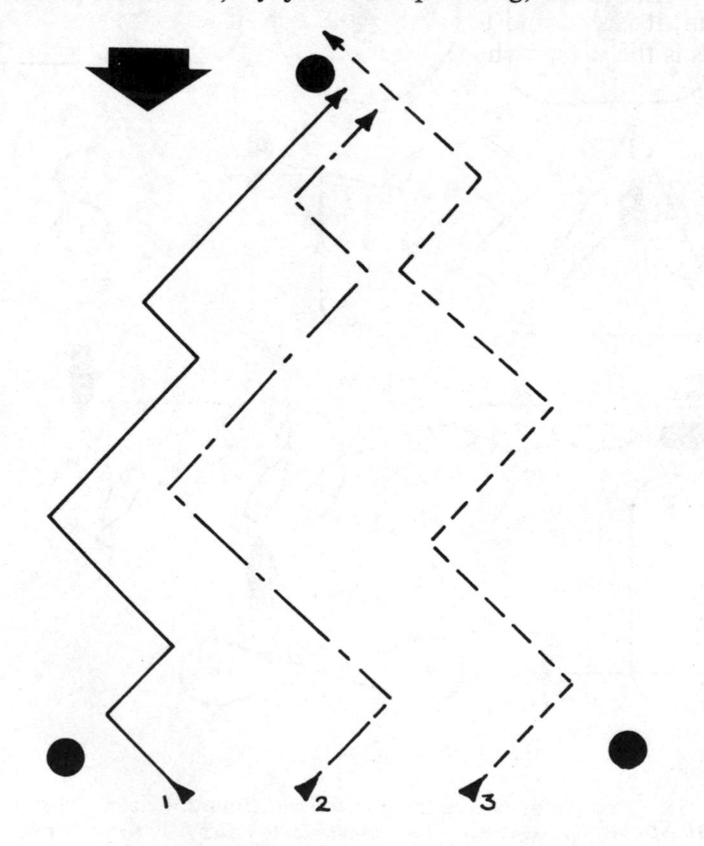

FIG. 52 Three alternative courses to the same point

could end on the favourable starboard-tack. The course made good is important but relies on very many variables. A helmsman should be prepared to cover a competitor's move and to keep between him and the next mark. He should avoid tacking duels and should not be 'dictated to' by a boat which is behind him.

Wind shifts should be acted upon, the boat should be driven at maximum speed. Once again, pointing ability is only required when in close proximity to other boats (for example in a luffing situation).

Fig. 53 shows a speed polar diagram which is a visual method of presenting the speed of a boat related to its heading, relative to the wind. With the help of such a diagram, it is possible to see the speed made good to windward. This is the factor which counts most on the windward leg.

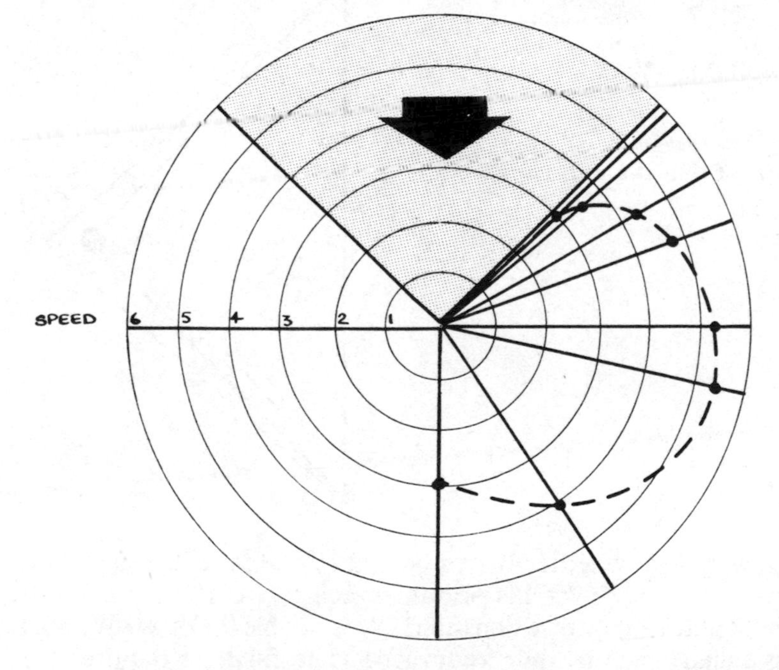

FIG. 53 The speed polar diagram

Boat Speed. All manner of exercises can be devised to make the pupil aware of what can be done to his boat and what his boat will do. The following exercise is used to demonstrate a boat's speed potential. The equipment required consists only of a watch, pencil and paper and three small markers. (A liquid soap bottle, sufficient string and half a brick does admirably!)

A windward position W is selected (Fig. 54) and a marker dropped. The boat is then sailed on a dead run for one minute. Marker D is dropped, and is now used as the starting point for a windward leg. The boat is sailed close-hauled, from leeward of D, until it is in a position when the helmsman judges that he can 'lay' W in one tack. Marker M is dropped, as the boat tacks, and the time is recorded when the boat reaches W (Fig. 55).

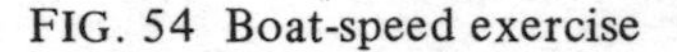
FIG. 54 Boat-speed exercise

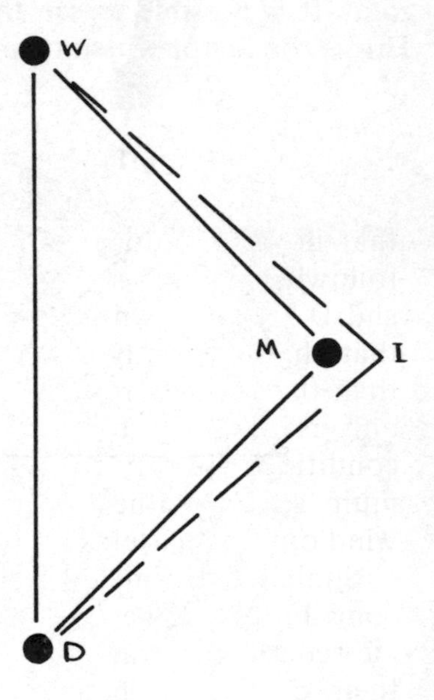

To gauge whether W can be laid in one tack, the helmsman should glance over his shoulder nearest to the stern of the boat, tacking only when mark W is visible. Course W, M, D is sailed and the time recorded. The final leg requires that the boat is sailed some five degrees free of the close-hauled position, to an imaginary buoy, I, situated outside the course which is being laid. Once again, the helmsman's judgement is important because, in effect, he is overstanding Mark W, so

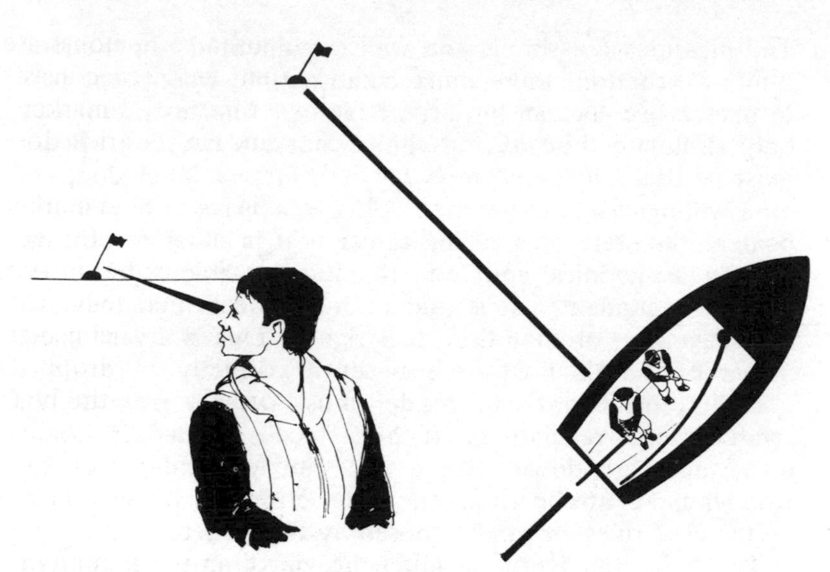

FIG. 55 Dropping a marker

that he can approach it five degrees off close-hauled. The following courses should now be compared; upwind D M W and D I W – downwind W D and W M D. It often happens that the apparently longer courses are as quick (or quicker) than the shortest routes. In the majority of classes, it is now universal practice to avoid sailing dead downwind unless the conditions are very rough and the boat is travelling at maximum speed. Otherwise downwind legs are sailed with the wind on the quarter.

Similar experiments to determine downwind tacking will contribute to a better understanding of the tactics. Groups blessed with a steady wind and sufficient time could produce their own speed polar diagram, by choosing a marker and sailing from it on a specific course, for one minute, before dropping their markers. The final pattern would give them a very good idea of the course which resulted in the best speed made good to windward.

Tuning the Boat. So much has been written concerning boat tuning that many people regard it as a 'black art'. There is no doubt that a boat must be tuned to improve performance.

The measures are simple and well documented. In the race training situation, there must come a time when boat performance becomes an important factor. The Instructor can only stimulate thought and show what can be done. Boats must be tuned *to* their crews *by* their crews. Much depends on a willingness to experiment. It oftens pays to buy an old boat at the start of a racing career – it is easier to bolt on the 'go-fast-goodies' and then to plug the holes when they become redundant! It is said of many boats that they are well balanced, or that they feel right. This is a very good indication that the boat has been set up correctly.

Hull, centreboard and rudder must be free from dents, scratches and irregularities. If the surface is painted, it should be given a rub down with a very fine wet-and-dry paper. Rudder and centreboard profile and section are either defined by the class rules, or can be chosen by the owner.

The hull should not be much heavier than the minimum class weight. Fittings should be kept to an absolute minimum. In the majority of dinghy fleets, the most successful boats have simple fittings. Many people see world-champion boats with a multiplicity of fittings, and then rush off to emulate them. They should pause to reflect that world-class crews need extremely sophisticated equipment for their type of competition. Their gear, often the prototype for future production, is made to suit their particular needs. Every piece of equipment must have a purpose, and must either make the crew's task easier or improve the boat's performance. It must also be possible to use equipment when the boat is being sailed hard. No gain will be derived from a piece of equipment which requires that the boat is stopped before it can be adjusted.

It is not possible to list *all* the 'variables', but attention to all or some of the following points may (probably will) affect performance: spinnaker hoisting, stowage and sheeting; main-sheet system and traveller; fairleads, their adjustment and cleating; sitting-out aids, adjustable footstraps and trapezes: centreboard hoist and retaining tackles; *and*, last but not least, the mast, its supports and the sails which are set upon it.

The mast, rigging and sails offer the greatest chance to the expert 'tuner'. Mast and sails should be 'made for each other'.

Sails are not simple pieces of triangular cloth to be stuck on any old piece of wood or metal! Jibs and mainsails are, nowadays, equipped with stretch luffs, downhauls, uphauls and outhauls. Mast and boom are tapered, have great pieces pared off, and are given 'bend' characteristics which suit the majority of conditions. The list will continue to grow. But there must come a time when the mast and sails will be tuned to perfection by a few, and will be gadget-ridden for the many. Mast-tuning involves controlling the fore-and-aft rake. A boat generally goes better downwind with the mast raked forward, and upwind with it raked aft. Its sideways bend must be controlled with spreaders or diamond wires. The newcomer is advised to experiment first with mast rake: then with the bend of the mast: then with the sails, fitting adjustments which will make them full in light airs, flatter in heavy weather. Kicking straps should be given special attention. They should be efficient and have a good reduction ratio and should be constantly adjusted, to suit conditions.

Finishing Well. Having dealt with some of the factors which assist a boat to the finishing line it only remains for the boat to sail across – or does it? Finishing needs as much careful consideration as starting, but unfortunately in a race there is very little time to size up the finishing position. The line is there, and has to be crossed in the most efficient manner. There may be competitors in front or behind, it is possible to lose or gain many places. The situation is further complicated by the fact that the crews are tired and unobservant and may have a fixation for a particular position on the line, irrespective of wind direction.

Practice finishes should be arranged using oblique lines which are constantly varied to wind direction. The boats should start in line abreast, some fifty yards from a turning mark and should have seventy-five yards to the finish. Fig. 56 shows two group-training finishes which have been used with much success. Fig. 57 is not recommended, but is quite common, in clubs with restricted waters. Helmsmen should be reminded that it is often quicker to reach towards the line, rather than run. Once again we are training sailors to be

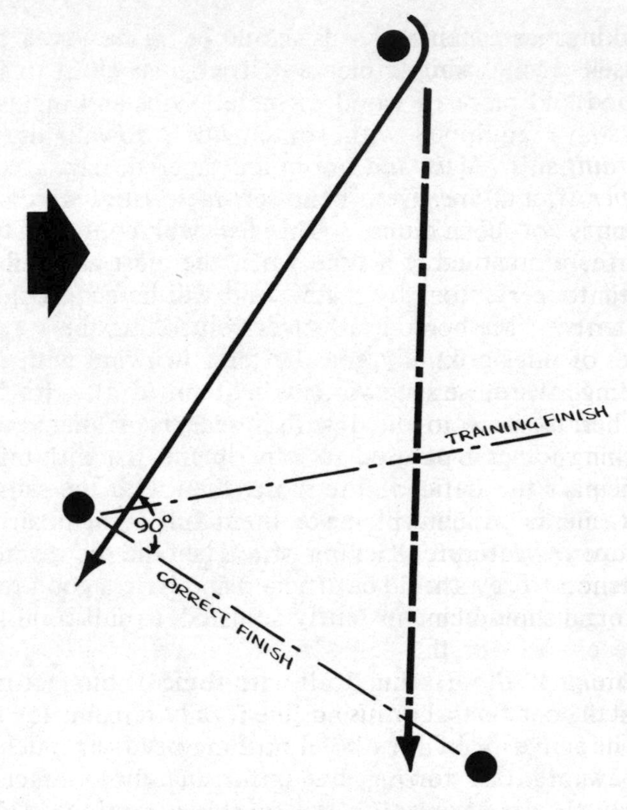

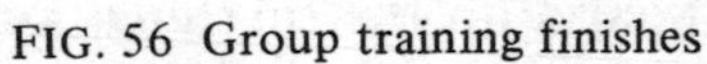
FIG. 56 Group training finishes

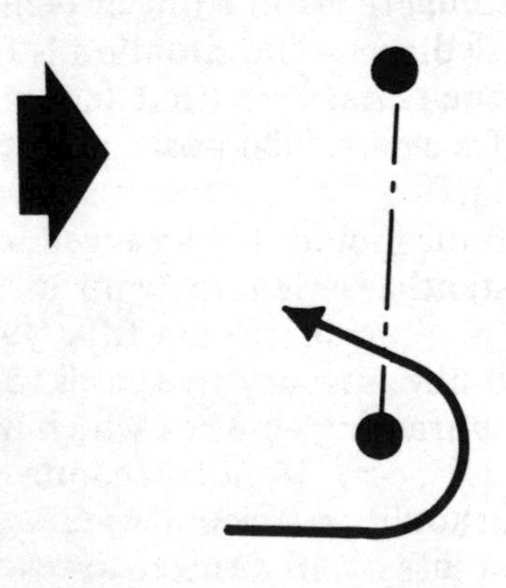

FIG. 57 Difficult training finish

thinking helmsmen rather than sheep. A man who thinks to himself 'I shall wait until someone else tries it' deserves to be second!

Learning to Organise Racing

Proper Management. The proper management of yacht racing is set out in detail in RYA booklet YR 3. It should, of course, be studied in detail. However, there are many important points to raise with the beginner in mind and the contents of the booklet are therefore not included within the pages of this book. Perhaps they should be recommended for reading after close study of this chapter.

There is more to the organisation of successful racing than working to a set pattern. Races are the responsibility of the Principal Race Officer and his staff.

Racing helmsmen are bound by a set of rules, many of which are open to interpretation and are dependent upon conflicting evidence from other crews. The Race Officer is responsible for organising racing in such a way as to ensure that there is little chance for the rules to be exploited. He should also ensure that those taking part are not put into unnecessarily difficult positions, because of his lack of planning.

The majority of sports have a referee, to see that penalties are awarded for fouls, or to make decisions concerning the rules. Sailors have only themselves and their sense of sportsmanship.

It is acknowledged that fierce international competition has sometimes led to racing which does not have such a high regard for the rules.

Many sailors seek constantly to change the rules to suit their own ends. This is an unhappy state of affairs, because the same spirit may spread down to club racing and thus destroy the enjoyment of many thousands of weekend sailors.

As they stand, the racing rules are basically sound, for such a complicated sport. Race officers must ensure that they are strictly observed.

Competitors should not hesitate to 'protest' another boat which is seen to infringe the rules; helmsmen who constantly cheat and 'get away with it', will become more daring; other competitors, seeing them 'get away with it', will follow them. Yacht racing will be the poorer for it.

Some Race Officers are in great demand, because competitors know that races under their control are 'no-nonsense' affairs, with well-laid starts and courses, which give every competitor a fair chance.

Race Officer Training. There is a great need for more trained Race Officers, especially as racing fleets expand. It is not enough that racing is carried out, it should be run in a competent manner. Unfortunately, there are many sailors who will never know the enjoyment to be derived from first-class race organisation. Many will move to other pastimes.

It has been found that Race Officers can be trained during race training exercises. There is much to be learned concerning the running of a race, but there is also scope for individual ideas.

Like the Race Officer himself, all his helpers are volunteers, people who have given up their time to organise and run a race or a championship. Some do so because they like it, some because they get satisfaction out of doing a job well, some because of pride in their club and a wish to gain prestige for it, some because they are enticed or interested, and some because they are pushed into service!

Most club members join in order to sail; very few join to put more in than they expect to take out.

To carry out the various duties needs certain skills, and there are not many clubs which can provide a really experienced team and reserves. Most clubs have to rely on some people to whom the whole operation is a mystery! This is particularly so in the provision of motor boats to act as rescue launches and to lay buoys. The standard of seamanship, and knowledge of coping with capsized boats, may leave much to be desired. The Race Officer must remember that he is dealing with volunteers who are doing their best. Often the Race Officer, at the start of a Championship week, has no idea who is expert and who is green, and he has little time in which to get them working as a team. It has to be very much of a team effort. The practice race is of far more benefit to the race officials than to the competitors.

No Race Officer is likely to forget the debt owed to all who make the races possible – the secretaries, the beach-master and his assistants, the caterers, launching parties, owners of committee boats and rescue launches, the recorders, gunner, time-keeper, signallers, wireless operators, messengers and all the rest – the Race Officer will not forget, but he could *well* remind a few competitors that the debt is never paid!

The Race Officials

The Race Officer. The safety record of sailing clubs is really quite remarkable. Throughout the British Isles the annual number drowned in sailing accidents is seldom more than half a dozen and these are usually visitors to the coast, not taking part in organised club activities. Race Officers can take a large slice of the credit for this record. With the vast number involved in the sport, it is an incredibly small total.

How is this record maintained? By preparation. Boats are designed to be manageable when capsized or full of water. Clubs insist on buoyancy rules being strictly adhered to: the buoyancy in every racing dinghy is inspected every year to see that it is secure and conforms to the rules. These boats are inspected by qualified buoyancy testers of whom there must be hundreds in the country besides all the official measures. The alert Race Officer, too, keeps his eyes open for infringements as he wanders around the boat park. Much is done, also, to encourage the use of lifejackets.

Dinghy sailors are put to considerable expense for safety's sake. So too, are the keel boat owners, with all the equipment which they are required to have, such as guard rails, inflatable dinghies, flares, navigation lights and equipment, extra anchors, etc. The majority of dinghy clubs run their own rescue boats, paid for and usually manned by club members. Sailing clubs have every right to be proud of their safety record.

The Race Officer in club races should take the lead in ensuring that the safety regulations are sufficient and he should carry out spot checks.

At dinghy open meetings he should detail someone to check buoyancy and the way it is secured in the boats of the fleet. He should also make sure that every boat has a valid certificate. He must know the general standard of safety in the fleet for he must decide whether to race or not, and this decision, often the most worrying of all, depends on so many different factors.

The rule says: 'It shall be the sole responsibility of the helmsman to decide whether to start or continue to race.' It relieves the Race Officer of any legal responsibility if someone is drowned. Nevertheless, it does not relieve him of his moral responsibilities, and these are far more important.

Since this saving clause was written into the rules, too many Race Officers hide behind it. Apparently they do not realise that less experienced competitors may not have enough knowledge to make a seamanlike judgement, yet this should not jeopardise the chances of those who are first-class sailors. The Race Officer must make a decision based on the facts.

He must take into consideration the class of boat; the general standard of seamanship, helmsmanship, weather forecasts from the Met Office; the tide and its probable effect on sea conditions; his own local weather prediction, the number of rescue boats available; visibility; temperature of wind and water; the efficiency of rescue crews and the type of launches; the speed with which conditions are changing. Above all he should be aware, as far as possible, of the quality of seamanship and helmsmanship in the fleet.

The Race Officer should be present when the sailing instructions are drafted so that he can make sure that heavy-weather courses are available; that there is a tally system or similar check, and so that he knows the wishes of the class association regarding length of course, type of course.

In club and championship races, he should know who are the weak links, those who may get into trouble. He should be able to warn the rescue boat coxswain about any competitors on whom he should keep a special watch.

To do all this he must know the local waters intimately and, if possible, be on the scene some hours before the event so that he can judge the speed of change in conditions.

This is most useful in cases where postponements are a possibility. It is not often possible to run a race later in the day, when it is blowing hard but it is worth a try, if there is any chance of the wind's moderating. In light airs it is often worth postponing, for the winds may well fill in from the sea.

When it is necessary to postpone because of weather conditions, it is far more satisfactory to postpone for, say, two hours than to keep the fleet hanging about afloat with half-hour delays.

One of the greatest safety factors is the choice of course in heavy weather. It should not be too long, for mental and physical fatigue can be dangerous and cold can be a killer. The course should not have reaches which are too broad, so that it is not possible to spill wind. Gybe marks can be arranged in calmer waters, or eradicated altogether, by having a figure-of-eight course. The course can be compact so that boats do several rounds, thereby keeping closer company than normally. This also gives the rescue boats a chance to be where they are needed.

When competitors are showing signs of fatigue, or the Race Officer knows from his own experience that they must be cold and tired, it may be prudent to shorten course. He must take into account the temperature of wind and water.

If every Race Officer instructed the coxswain of his rescue boat so that he could recognise the danger signals, he would be relieved, to some extent, of one of his greatest worries. In heavy weather, the number of capsizes usually follows a pattern. A few will capsize before the start – usually beginners or the inattentive. These are fresh and usually capable of fending for themselves. Several will probably capsize on the first planing reach or at the gybe mark – these are the less experienced or those with gear failure. This will have thinned out the fleet and there will probably be no more until near the end of the race when the mentally and physically tired crews will pay for their slower reactions. The Race Officer must remember that these crews are not fresh and will need watching closely. He should be able to judge from his own sailing experience what state of tiredness has been reached by competitors.

Lifejackets may have saved many a man from drowning but those who have been in the water can still suffer from heat loss and die as a result.

The Race Officer must bear in mind that lifejackets are intended to make sailing safer. They were never intended to entice the Race Officer to send boats out in unsuitable weather – in other words to take bigger risks. A responsibility is sometimes put on a Race Officer to hoist, or not to hoist, a signal requiring all competitors to wear lifejackets. If there is such a signal, then the checking of lifejackets is essential before the race.

The Timekeeper. The Race Officer has a lot on his mind. He should make sure his Timekeeper knows his job and keeps his mind on it and not on the scenery.

The clock should be checked for good timekeeping. Remember, the whole fleet is sitting with stopwatch in hand, just waiting for it to be one second out in five minutes. At least one other watch or clock must be synchronised with the master clock. The clock should be right but no great harm is done if it is a few seconds slow. It must never be fast.

The Timekeeper must know the timetable and give the Race Officer a countdown. If the start is from a committee boat, the Race Officer will have arranged to go aboard early. If he appears to be running late, the Timekeeper should remind him and keep him up to scratch. Reminders are also welcome at, say, one hour to the Start, half an hour to the Start, five minutes to the first gun, four, three, two, one, and half a minute to the gun, ten seconds to the gun and class flag. The Timekeeper should never say 'five!' – it is frequently mistaken for 'fire!' – and the gun goes! It is best, if this does happen, to have a General Recall.

Five seconds before any gun the Timekeeper should say: 'Stand by,' then: 'four, three, two, one, gun.'

Each minute should then be given with the usual countdown of seconds, stating what happens at the next gun, that is: 'Ten seconds to the Blue Peter' – 'Ten seconds to the Start.'

The information given should be repeated by the Race Officer to let the Timekeeper know that he has been heard, and heard correctly.

The Timekeeper must make a note of the actual time of start. He should time each round and report the elapsed time, if there is any likelihood of the race running near the time limit; the Race Officer then has the necessary information to help to decide whether to shorten course.

At the finish, the Timekeeper, in conjunction with Recorders, should time all boats.

For some reason, mistakes in timing are frequently made in the 33- and 38-minute area of the clock. Special care should be taken at these times.

The Signaller. The Signaller's job starts as soon as he knows where he is to operate. If from a clubhouse with a fixed flagstaff, there is probably little preparation to be done, except at the beginning of the season. Just a quick check to see that there are sufficient halyards, a complete set of code flags (and that they are in their correct pigeon-holes), and a clear mind as to the order of signals required.

On a committee boat, things may not be quite so straightforward. The boat, which has been lent for the occasion, may not have a suitable mast and it will be necessary to go aboard the day before to sort it out.

The mast is an important part of the Starting Line and should be large. Five halyards will be needed: one at the masthead, for the burgee or identification flag of the committee boat; one for the course flag; one for the class; one for Blue Peter; and a spare with the General Recall bent on ready.

A complete set of flags should be carried and kept in the flag locker until needed. Don't get out the ones you are going to need and make a separate pile of them – they nearly always get muddled up or kicked out of place (or even overboard).

The flags should be easily visible at about three quarters of a mile. The small flags frequently carried by yachts are useless except for dressing overall.

A check should be made to see that all flags are in their correct locker and that they are correctly rolled. A flag should be folded in four along the hoist with the identifying letter or number on the outside. The flag should then be bunched into the middle and then rolled, the identifying letter still on the outside, the tail passed a couple of times round the flag, and a bight tucked under ready for hoisting and breaking. When a flag has been correctly bunched up, the final effect will grip the sides of the locker and the flag will not fall out when the ship rolls. Even when ashore, flags should be kept thus.

If Race Officers would insist on using flag signals for controlling the fleet, helmsmen would learn at least some of them. It can be educational and acts as an introduction to the customs of the sea.

There are times, however, when other methods are used because of local conditions, such as when a club is starting from a fixed line at right angles to a lee shore. Then the helmsmen *never* learn to read the flags.

Halyards, when not in use, should be clipped together. The clips should be about eighteen inches above the rail or cleat. This makes it easy to tell which is the hoist and which the downhaul and which clip to use for the top of the flag. Halyards should never be belayed with the clips below the cleat. Flags must never be hoisted upside down! They cannot be hoisted hard up if they are. Not for an instant should one end of a halyard be allowed to hang free – it will be at the yardarm before you can grab it.

Two sets of clips on the same halyard can be used to advantage, where several classes or changes of course are needed in quick succession – the next class flag being bent onto the bottom clip while the current flag is flying.

Care should be taken in choosing a suitable halyard. For instance, a pennant should not be flown close to windward of a flag, for fear that it may mask the flag. The Blue Peter should be flown where it cannot ever be masked. The pennant can be dipped to clear the flag but the Blue Peter must be broken hard up.

The Signaller should be equipped with correct shapes for postponement purposes. He should, also, make himself familiar with all the special signals regarding postponements; five-minute rule; general recall; 'come within hail'; cancellations; abandonment; distress; correct use of ensign, etc. He should never belay halyards too tightly when they are dry; they may break when it rains.

The Gunner should check that he has two, preferably three, guns in working order. He must see that there is plenty of ammunition of the right bore and that it has not swollen with dampness. He will require a ramrod, preferably one which does not require him to put his hand in front of the muzzle. He will also need lashings, to tie the guns to prevent them going overboard, if he is operating on a committee boat.

He must position his guns so that none of the starting or finishing crew can possibly get in front of them.

On many occasions the committee boat will be surrounded by sails, some over the line and others not. If there is likelihood of injury or damage, the gunner should not fire. It is a small matter to have a General Recall, if it is necessary. He should not fire so long as there is any danger to life or property and he must be the sole judge, for the Race Officer will be watching the line. The same, of course, applies to guns at the finish. Failure to fire the gun does not invalidate the start, for the visual signal is the one that matters.

In the case of a misfire, the next gun should be fired *if this can be done immediately* but, if there is going to be a delay of a second or so, the other gun should not be fired. It will only be misleading.

Recall guns should be fired at about three-second intervals. This is also a reasonable interval for guns for 'Shortened Course' or 'Race Abandoned'.

Guns should not be loaded until shortly before use and, of course, should always be put away unloaded. The Race Officer should check that this is done.

The Committee Boat Crew. The Race Officer must make a fairly rapid assessment of the proficiency and seamanship of those handling the committee boat. She must be handled with precision, and anchored so as to lie exactly as the Race Officer wants it. This is by no means easy, with wind and tide in opposition, but it can be done.

When anchoring, the depth, and quality of holding ground, must, of course, be known. Once the anchor is holding, it is best to drop back a boat's length or two so that, when final adjustments are made to the boat's position, she can be brought forward without risk of dragging. It may be necessary to keep the engine ticking over, especially when using chain. If the boat is driven to leeward by a gust, the chain will tighten and, when the gust has gone, the weight of chain sinking to the bottom will give considerable forward way to the boat. This movement is not nearly so marked if warp is used. It may be necessary to sheer the boat one way or the other. This can easily be done by taking a line from about twenty yards out on the cable and heaving in aft.

It is sometimes advantageous to drop a stern anchor only.

The skipper should be asked to take cross bearings when the boat has settled, and to watch for, and report, any dragging.

If there is a choice, pick a boat with a reliable engine which will give a minimum of five knots with a head sea.

Committee boats are often far too big for the job. So often the boat should be moved a short distance but, being cumbersome, the Race Officer is likely to leave it where it is to save trouble and delay, when he knows he could set a better starting or finishing line. Large committee boats have a habit of acquiring several more people than are really necessary. Unemployed chatterers can be a harassment to those with a specific job to do.

The Recorders. The Recorder's first job is to get an up-to-the-minute list of entries. In normal club racing, there is often no written list of entrants. Numbers can be taken as they are seen in the starting area. As soon as they have started, the number of boats starting in the class should be counted and checked with the number of sail numbers recorded, to make sure you have the lot. The time of the start should also be recorded – this may be needed if there is, for example, a time limit.

In open meetings and championships, where there is a definite entry list, the sail numbers should be typed out on a single sheet and, as the boats come to the starting area, the sail numbers should be 'ticked off' as they are seen.

At the weather mark first time round, it is unlikely that the committee boat will be in time to get the early numbers (as she should not plough through the fleet). These will have to be taken by recorders on another launch and handed to the committee boat as soon as possible.

The Race Officer should station a boat where the Recorders can see the numbers easily as the boats round the mark. Sail numbers and at least *some* times should be recorded in chronological order. When all the boats have rounded the mark, the sail numbers should be read back, and a mark made against the numbers on the entry list. This must be done on every round. It is the only way of making sure that every boat has sailed the right number of rounds. In big fleets, particularly in extremes of weather, boats can easily be lapped, by sailing into a flat spot or capsizing, and this can cause chaos unless the Recorders are prepared.

If there is more than one class racing, no attempt should be made to separate them until they have all finished.

With large fleets, or where there are many boats finishing in quick succession, or when sail numbers are difficult to read because of the angle of the sail, there should be at least two recording teams. Each team should consist of three people: one calling the number, one writing down – if possible with occasional times – and one watching and listening for any errors or missed numbers. He can either interrupt then, or make a note for later correction.

A fair copy should be made of the result for each class and posted on the appropriate notice board. Declaration sheets must be checked and the results amended as necessary. Results of protests and such matters as failure to produce certificates, or no tally, must also be recorded.

The Rescue Boat Crews. Before deciding to allow racing, the Race Officer should satisfy himself as to rescue boats; the number, quality and size of boats and crew.

Normally it is better to have the heavier boats at the leeward end of the course. They can punch their way to windward better than the light runabout type which are best used on the fast-reaching legs.

It must be made quite plain to the crews that they are there to protect life and must not get involved in slow salvage work, nor are they there to act as Press launch, or to take passengers.

The crews must be made familiar with the best way to cope with various situations – boats with broken rudders; burst buoyancy bags; built-in-buoyancy full of water; masts stuck in the mud, etc.

They must be ever-vigilant and treat as urgent any capsized boat when the crew is not visible. They must treat as urgent any sign of exhaustion, particularly on cold days. Any boat capsizing several times should have an attentive eye kept on it. Most of the time it will be a case of standing by and keeping clear, but the skilled rescue boat skipper, probably a club member, and therefore knowledgeable about the boats and the crews, should be quick to detect real trouble and be able to get close in before it happens.

The time may come when he must *order* the competitor to abandon his boat and get aboard the rescue launch.

It is often the case that competitors, possibly in an exhausted condition, are reluctant to do this and it must be made clear that the rescue boat skipper has the final power to over-ride the natural inclination to stay with the boat.

Every official launch should be properly equipped. Such equipment should include an extra anchor and warp and Flag M (in case a mark is sunk or breaks adrift). Apart from this equipment it is advisable to carry a few spare buckets, means of attracting attention and all the obvious gear normally carried by prudent seamen, especially if operating in sea areas.

Rescue boats should not, of course, be kept on patrol, if it is not necessary. In light airs, the heavy boats can probably be brought in or anchored if it is clear that they are not needed.

Clubs, if they can afford it, can arrange licences to use radio communications. Details of the requirements are available from the RYA.

The Beachmaster. The Race Officer relies on this man for shoreline organisation. He is responsible for the allocation of berths, for boat parking and for keeping competitors informed and, in some cases, for keeping the local council happy.

The Race Officer and the Beachmaster liaise on all the race arrangements, both before the race and after it is over:

the launching parties; buoyancy inspections; recovery of boats; measurement of boats; examination of certificates; checking boats without tallies; missing boats; calling additional help; and publication of results and points. Immediately after the start, the Beachmaster should tell the committee boat what boats are still ashore and which tallies have not been taken.

Running the Racing

Points to Watch. Clubs may be lucky enough to have a regular Race Officer and team and regular rescue launch coxswain. They get to know one another, and racing seldom presents any real problems. For instance, a Race Officer can risk giving a certain course if he knows the rescue coxswain is a good seaman, and is competent. When the Race Officer has complete confidence in his assistants, much of the worry is taken out of the job. He can concentrate on picking the most interesting courses and pay more attention to weather conditions, leaving the mechanics of starting and finishing races to his team mates.

Little need be said to explain how a normal race is started. A warning gun, a preparatory gun and a starting gun. This is simple enough.

It is when things won't go quite to plan that some get flustered. An error in timing, for instance. Remember it is the visual signal which counts. If you have made a mistake, admit it, have a General Recall and get it right. Far better than to sail the race, only to have to declare it void in the end. Be careful never to start a race before its scheduled time. Stick to the sailing instructions, if possible, and avoid relying on alterations pinned on notice boards. Sooner or later, someone will say he never saw it. If this has to be done, see that some signal is written into the sailing instructions which says – All helmsmen to collect special instructions from Clubhouse' – one or two will, and they will probably tell the rest who won't bother – but that is then up to them. This way out of trouble can be used for practically any emergency. If, for instance, you find someone has lost the Blue Peter, don't get fussed. Hoist Flag L (or whatever your sailing instructions say) and then tell them (in writing if they want it so) what signal will replace P. This could be another flag, a shape or even the signaller's trousers! But competitors should have it in writing.

How late can a boat start? A starter must sail about in the vicinity of the starting line between the preparatory and starting signals. Pretty ambiguous. How close is 'vicinity'? Is being anchored in a strong tide and no wind 'sailing about'? When is it legal for a committee boat, forming one end of a starting line, to leave station for the windward mark? These are points which should be settled by the Race Officer with due regard for his standards of fairness. There is always a right of appeal for someone who feels aggrieved.

The Race Officer can have a General Recall, if there are a number of *unidentified* premature starters. He should not have a General Recall because there are a lot of boats over the line (or even the whole fleet) but *only* if he is unable to identify them. This is a point which is often overlooked. It is sometimes easier to take the sail numbers of the boats starting correctly and disqualify the rest. Sometimes it may be fair to make a deliberate mistake, and have a General Recall.

When there are many classes, the starting team must work to a set method (or get in a hopeless muddle!). Rather than prolong the starts, classes are often sent off at five-minute intervals.

The method which seems to cause the least confusion is to treat the starting gun for one class as the preparatory gun for the next (that is, five minutes before their start) and hoist the Blue Peter three minutes before the start. With halyards with two pairs of Inglefield clips, the next class flag, and any change of course, can be bent on at the bottom, and hoisted automatically as the others are hauled down.

Sail numbers of starters are recorded, and the boats counted just after the start as a check that all sail numbers have been taken; then the sail numbers of the next class and so on, keeping an eye for boats retiring from the earlier classes.

At the finish, every boat must be timed in, in chronological order, in one long list. The sail numbers on the starters' list should be crossed off, so that, as soon as the rescue boat returns, there is a list of missing boats immediately available.

Although figure-of-eight courses are rather frowned on by the RYA, it is well to have them among the alternatives for use in very heavy weather. In club racing, too, the more variety in the courses, the more competitors will learn and enjoy their racing. Courses must be chosen carefully (on the day) to suit tidal and weather conditions, with particular regard to fog, bearing in mind the lack of experience of some of the beginners, both young and old. They need encouragement, not punishment.

Laying the Starting Line. Of all the jobs for those running the racing, this is the most spectacular, and the one which will bring most criticism. A good starting line will get the fleet away to a good-tempered start. Other considerations are just as important but seem to escape the attention of most competitors.

The line should be designed to give every boat in the fleet a chance to be in the front rank at the start, and even expert helmsmen must be encouraged to use the full length of the line.

The Race Officer must first find the direction of the wind. One method is to tie a yard of cotton to the forestay of the committee boat, at about head height. Using a hand-bearing compass, a very accurate direction can be obtained. Any indicator placed higher on the boat is subject to a lot of rolling. It is advisable to have an anemometer to record the wind strength. This can help a later decision to shorten course.

It must appear to helmsmen that one end of the line is as good as the other. Set the line basically at right-angles to the wind, which should be blowing exactly from the direction of the first mark. Other things being equal, this would give a slight advantage to boats starting at the starboard end of the line. They can tack when they wish. Such a line would tend to have a large bunch at the starboard end. To obviate this, it should be given a few degrees of port bias. However, on a line long enough for a big fleet, conditions are almost certain to be different at opposite ends. The advantages (or disadvantages) of tide must be taken into account. This must be considered very carefully. The Race Officer must make allowance for the fact that a boat with a lee-bowing tide, particularly in light airs, can have a tremendous advantage over the one with a weather-bowing tide. The advantage decreases as the wind increases. With the tide running along the line, this will require a major adjustment to the basic line. The proximity, or otherwise, of tidal advantages beyond the starting area must also be taken into account.

The effect of land near the course will differ on sunny and cloudy days. It may well cause wind deflection which could make one end of the line advantageous. So, too, may cloud formations and the natural tendency of the wind to veer or back. Another major consideration is, of course, possible changes of weather.

When the Race Officer has calculated all these variables, he will be able to decide on a fair angle of the line and, with luck, competitors will be undecided as to which is the better end and thus tend to use its full length. It is more important that competitors should think the line is fair than that it should be fair! An inexperienced fleet will usually crowd the starboard end of the line, and extra bias must be used to spread them along it.

Deciding on the length of the line is always a problem. In heavy weather, boats need room to manoeuvre safely. With a weather-going tide, they are likely to be early for the start and want room to bear away. A long line will give every boat a chance to get clear wind and will obviate any bumping and boring with its consequent fraying of tempers. Everyone can then start in a happier frame of mind. Twice the total length of boats competing should be about the limit. Too long a line magnifies any error the Race Officer may have made in its angle and also increases the competitors' difficulty in knowing its exact location.

On a short line, which will be crowded, the 'clever' boys, if they have made a bad start themselves, may deliberately cause a General Recall by forcing as many boats as possible over the line. This is far less likely to happen if there is plenty of room to manoeuvre. Generally, however, it is safe to assume that nobody wants to be over the line if he can possibly help it. The starting discipline of the fleet may vary in different classes, but it is generally pretty high.

Another problem is to let competitors know just where the line is. The chances are that it is impossible for a helmsman to get any satisfactory transit, for committee boats can sheer about a lot, depending on the depth of water and the relative directions and strength of wind and tide.

There is no rule that the committee boat must be at the starboard end of the line – in fact, just before the start, most helmsmen are looking towards the port end of the line, and it helps them to have a better transit at the end.

The line should be as clear as possible. A fast, light motor boat can be used to mark the line near the centre, until a few seconds before the start.

Another way which has worked successfully is to lay a buoy in the middle of the line to act merely as a transit mark. It is kept exactly on the line by pivoting the line on the buoy. This means that, if the Race Officer wishes to change the angle, he can haul up or drop back on his anchor. The launch marking the other end can do the same to keep the committee boat's mast and the buoy in transit. By this means, all boats can have a transit to let them know just where the line is.

It may be necessary, when starting large fleets, to invoke one or other of the special starting rules, such as the so-called one-minute rule, if competitors are likely to block one another's sight of the transit thereby making a General Recall practically a certainty.

Whatever is done it must be written into the sailing instructions.

Race Officers can invoke the 'Round the Ends' rule provided in IYRU rule 51.1 (c).

Alternatively, although not recommended for important races, the one-minute rule can be used to good effect. This reads as follows:

'When any part of a yacht's hull, crew or equipment is over the starting line or its extensions, during the minute before her starting signal is made, she shall be disqualified;
Note: The beginning of this period may be indicated by a flag and sound signal different in character from the sound signals for starting, in which case the sailing instructions should so state.

'The period may be altered from one minute, but one

minute is recommended. Also this rule can be varied to read:

'"Any yacht which either is within or enters the triangular area, the base of which shall be the starting line or as defined in the sailing instructions, and the apex of which shall be the first mark, during the minute before her starting signal is made shall be disqualified."'

For club racing it is, in fact, often very useful to alter the period from one minute to five. The main object is, as stated, to avoid the irritation of a General Recall.

Another method of starting a large fleet is illustrated in Fig 58. Known as the 'Gate Start' it gives nobody an advantage. The lead boat runs down a pre-determined line, close-hauled on the port tack, followed by the committee boat. People may start astern of the committee boat.

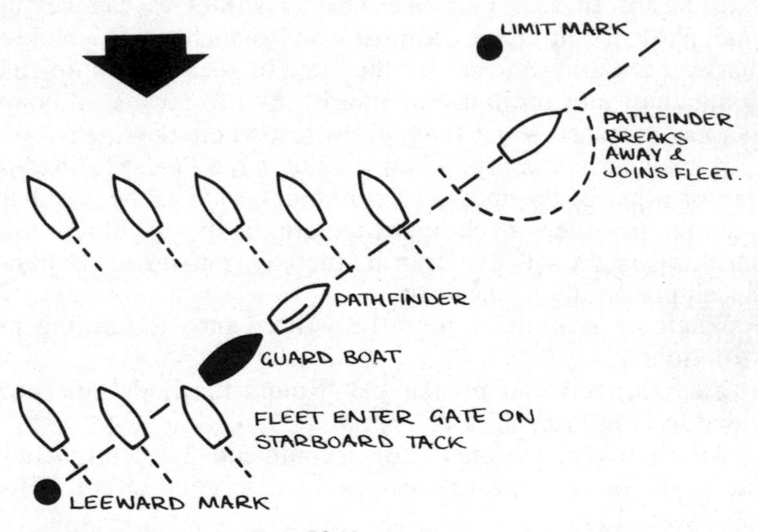

FIG. 58 A gate start

Laying the Finishing Line. The course is usually finished at the windward mark. The finishing line should be at right angles to the wind and can usually be quite short, say 100 yards or less. The committee boat should anchor outside the triangle and hoist a Blue Flag or shape when she is on station.

If the course is being shortened at some other mark or,

because of windshifts, the boats are finishing on a reach or run, the line should be at right-angles to the last leg sailed.

If the course is being shortened, Flag S must be flown and two guns fired. Competitors should be given as much warning as possible but it is no good firing guns unless the boats are near enough to be quite certain that the signal is intended for them.

On all finishing lines with a lot of boats racing, whether on Olympic-type courses or fixed club lines, a boat with Recorders aboard should be stationed beyond the opposite end to the committee boat. Frequently the Race Officer is unsighted by a sail or boats may finish so close that the Recorders on the committee boat are unable to cope. A double check is invaluable.

The Race Officer must watch very carefully when a boat finishes. She is still subject to the rules until she has cleared the line, either by crossing it or dropping back and clearing. She finishes when any part of her hull, crew or equipment in its usual position (even the top of the mast) crosses the line.

It must be crossed from the direction of the last mark. The sailing instructions should be very carefully worded to see that the line cannot legally be crossed from the wrong side and then recrossed. The Race Officer must bear in mind the extended time limit and make the appropriate signal if there are still boats which have not retired.

Laying Marks. In club racing, the marks used are usually left down for the season and are therefore fairly substantial and, for financial reasons, are usually moored with heavy sinkers and good chain. As they are being used by competitors who know the waters and the positions of the buoys, they do not necessarily have to be as clearly visible as those used for open meetings or Championship races.

It is preferable not to have a ring or topmark to which boats can tie up. Seasonal buoys are often dragged out of position by fishing boats tying up to them. They should be painted one colour only. Stripes only tend to camouflage them.

Buoys for specially laid courses, however, are a different

matter. These have several special requirements. Visibility is of the utmost importance. Single colour, therefore, and bright yellow for preference. It must be easily carried in small fast boats and be simple to moor. The answer seems to be an inflatable sphere about five feet in diameter. This has several advantages. Firstly it can be seen equally well from any direction. It is all visible, it draws about two inches, it is light and easily carried ashore and afloat. Drawing so little, there is a minimum of tidal drag, so ground tackle can be reduced to a light anchor and thin line. No damage is done to boat or buoy if it is hit. It can be deflated for storage purposes.

The more conventional marks rely on flags or topmarks and are not so convenient. A topmark requires something heavier below water to keep it upright. This puts the buoy lower in the water – more tidal drag – heavier tackle – more trouble to lay and move and store.

CHAPTER SIX

Advanced Boat-Handling Techniques

TRAPEZING

One of the earliest known forms of trapezing was the use of ropes attached to the hounds of the mast of Beecher Moore's Thames A rater. These ropes were known as bell ropes, and the crew (sitting out in a normal position) held on to these ropes in order to support themselves. The first recorded form of trapeze which allowed the crew to stand on the side of the gunwale was the trapeze used by Peter Scott in his International 14 when he won the Prince of Wales Cup. The suspension point was high up on the chest, and the belt was fixed underneath the arms. The trapezing system that we know today, with the crew supported at approximately his centre of gravity, appeared at the IYRU two-man centre-boarder trials, which introduced such boats as the Flying Dutchman, 505 and Osprey. Various refinements in actual fittings have taken place since that time, but the principle has remained exactly the same.

Boat Fittings

Most mast manufacturers provide an attachment on the mast for the trapeze wire, but most crews prefer to attach them to the shroud. The trapeze wire should be 5/64 diameter, 1 x 19 stainless steel wire which should be 'talurited' directly to the trapeze handle; the height of the handle being approximately two feet above the gunwale. The type of handle to use is illustrated in Fig. 59. It is easier and safer to use than many other types.

There are a number of different arrangements for attaching the trapeze rings to the handles. In order to avoid confusion only two of the types commonly in use are described here.

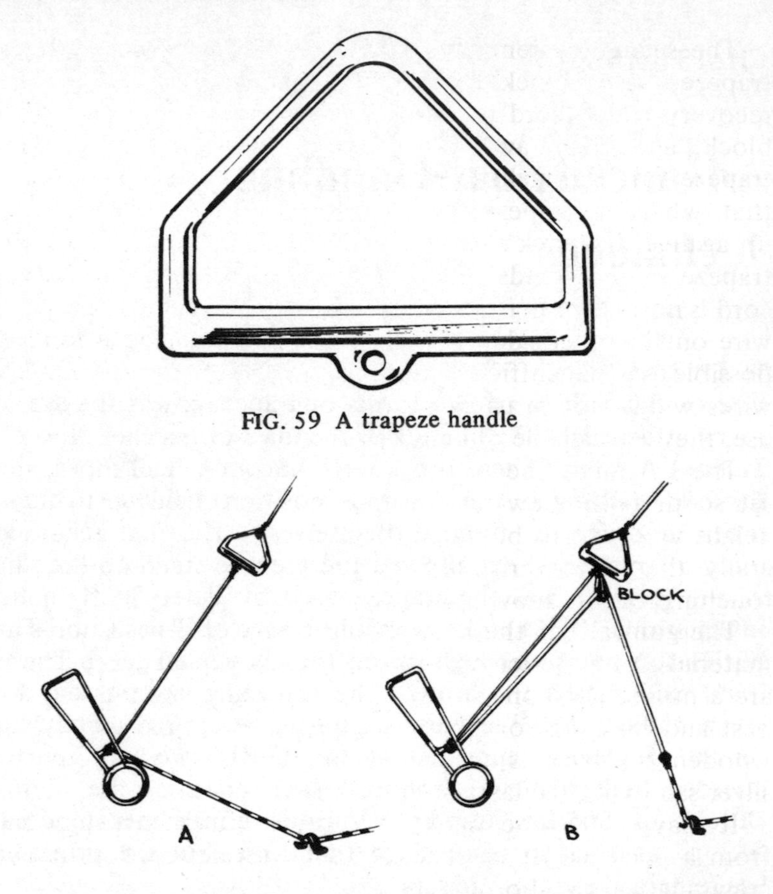

FIG. 59 A trapeze handle

FIG. 60 Two methods of fixing the trapeze wire to the handle

Fig. 60a shows the fixed variety. The trapeze wire is retained in the boat by a shock cord taken from the centre bar of the trapeze ring, through a lead on the deck of the boat. This should be positioned at least six inches away from the shrouds, and out of the line of the jib. This system, excellent for advanced racing, nearly always means that, when the crew comes back into the boat, the trapeze ring automatically frees itself from the trapeze belt (unless the belt is fitted with a retaining catch). The crew does not have to worry about unfastening the trapeze wire when tacking quickly.

The second system, which is ideal for teaching people to trapeze, has a block fixed to the handle (Fig. 60b). The recovery shock cord is attached to a rope led through this block, and taken away through a lead on the boat. The trapeze ring is attached to the end of the rope. This means that, when the trapeze is not in use, the trapeze ring is held up against the block clear of the deck; when hooked onto the trapeze belt, it tends to stay hooked on. The return shock cord is normally run round, and across, the boat to the trapeze wire on the other side. This elastic should be made as long as possible, so that sufficient tension can be kept on the trapeze wires whilst not in use, and, alternatively, when they are in use, they are capable of being extended easily.

The height of the trapeze ring above the deck should be set so that the crew trapezes in a horizontal position. The height will have to be altered to suit individual crews. Generally the bottom ring of the trapeze link should be just touching, or just above the deck.

The gunwale of the boat should be covered with non-slip material along the length where the crew will trapeze. There are a number of non-slip materials available. In practice, the best and cheapest form of non-slip, which can be applied to wooden gunwales, is obtained by mixing a small quantity of silver sand with the last coat of varnish.

It may be found easier to trapeze if the jib sheets are led from a position aft of the normal trapezing position of the crew. 'Jammers' should be positioned in the boat to take the jib sheet, and it is of the utmost importance that it should be easy to release the sheets from these 'jammers' when trapezing. A compromise has often to be reached when considering the position of the 'jammers'. Even if the helmsman has to lend a hand to jam the sheet, the primary consideration should be the ability to free the sheet easily.

Trapeze Belts and Clothing

The trapeze belt should be one which has webbing between the legs. This type is, in fact, more comfortable than those constructed of cloth. It is also definitely longer-wearing. If it is necessary to replace the webbing, it is very easily done. The shoulder straps should be fastened so that they cannot fall off the shoulders. In most production trapeze belts, these straps are tied together, fairly near to the shoulders, and when fastening them, they should be crossed at the front. The shoulder straps should be tensioned so that the wearer can comfortably touch his hands together with his arms stretched above his head.

Lifejackets, if worn, should be worn over the top of the trapeze belt. Various types of jacket are on the market which allow the hook of the trapeze belt to remain clear.

When it comes to choosing clothes, every effort should be made to reduce the amount of windage of the crew when on the trapeze. Loose clothing should be avoided. Various all-in-one suits, in very lightweight material, are available. If these are worn over the top of normal sailing clothes, they help to keep the windage to a minimum. The shoes used by the crew should be tight-fitting and of the non-slip variety.

Trapezing Techniques

When trapezing for the first time, the biggest mistake made by most people is to stand on the gunwale, and *then* go out on the trapeze wire. The whole secret of trapezing is, first of all, to sit out over the side of the boat on the trapeze wire. Once the wire becomes tight between the hook and the mast, it is a very simple matter to move out over the gunwale into the normal trapezing position. The actual procedure for reaching this position is given below.

The trapeze ring is clipped to the trapeze belt and the hand is then run along the trapeze system to the handle, keeping tension on the lower part of the trapeze system. The hand is then swung out over the shoulder, until the trapeze wire becomes tight between the handle and the mast. Keeping tension on this arm, ease out backwards into a position similar to that adopted when using toe straps. The forward foot is brought up to the gunwale, then the crew can swing out on the trapeze wire, bringing out the rear foot last. The height of the trapeze wire should be such that he trapezes horizontally with the weight taken on the balls of the feet, legs slightly apart and knees slightly bent. If the shoulder straps have adjusted properly, these should provide support to the back. If they are too loose, there will be no support, and if they are too tight, they will cause the crew to double up.

The man on the trapeze must keep his knees flexible and move with the movement of the boat. His feet should be approximately eighteen inches apart. If they are any closer, he will tend to fall off as the boat moves over the waves. If his feet are further apart, it becomes impossible, when any violent motion takes place, to make corrections to avoid being thrown off.

When the wind dies, he should reduce his effective righting moment by bending the knees, as this rapidly reduces the distance of his centre of gravity from the gunwale. The usual mistake when the wind does die away is to grab hold of the handle, which increases the tendency for the boat to be pulled down on top of the crew.

On a trapeze the crew can rapidly change the trim of the craft by moving forward or aft. On a sliding seat he cannot do this.

When it is necessary to come in off the trapeze, the procedure is exactly the reverse of that adopted in getting out on the wire.

There are far too many pictures of crew with hands extended above the head. It is not a recommended position for trapezing for any length of time. The main mistake made by beginners is to trapeze with the head held forward. If the head is held back, it will considerably help to increase the righting moment of the boat. Hands should be kept down by the side of the body, or *one* hand held at the back of the head to support it. There is no need, except when getting on or off the trapeze wire, to hold the handle.

Training

If it is possible, set up a dry-land training system. A bench can be used to represent the side of the boat, with a convenient eye on a building from which to hang the trapeze wire. Pupils should then be taught to get on and off the trapeze wire, using the techniques described. At first, each position should be dealt with separately then, after two or three attempts, these will flow together and make the action continuous.

SPINNAKER HANDLING

Many articles have been written about the use of the spinnaker, but most of them assume that the reader has a basic knowledge of spinnaker techniques.

There are, of course, many techniques for spinnaker handling and it is impossible to describe all of them. One system is described which can be developed to suit individual boats and crews and which, it is hoped, will be readily understandable by novice pupils. It must be emphasised, at this stage, that there is no substitute for practice or development. If fittings do not work or are in the wrong place, change them! Spinnaker handling is easy if everything, including the crew, works properly.

Basic Theory

In order to use a spinnaker efficiently, it is necessary to understand the basic theory of the air flow across the spinnaker. We will examine this flow in two conditions: first, when dead running, and then on a reach.

Fig. 61 shows the air flow on a dead run. The wind flows into and down the spinnaker. A small part of the air flow escapes round the side of the spinnaker. It is very easy when

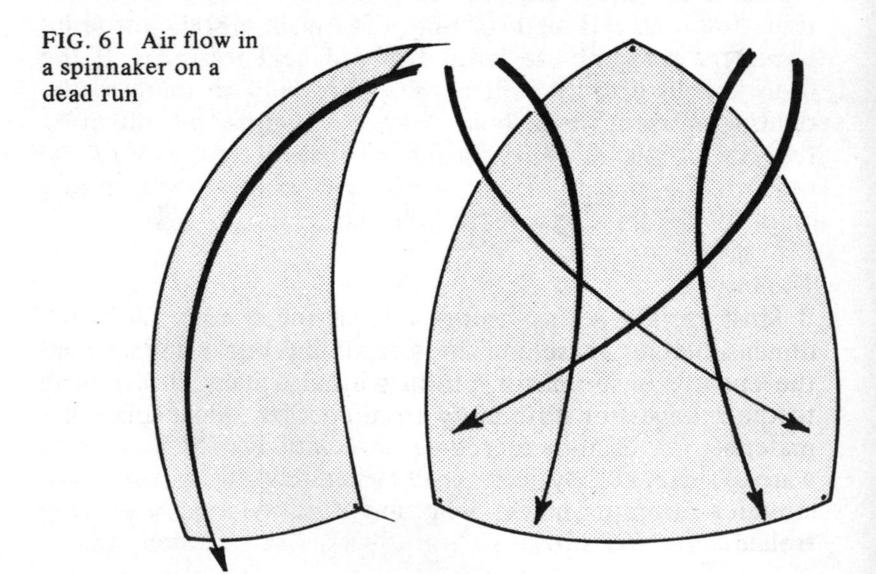

FIG. 61 Air flow in a spinnaker on a dead run

dead running for a spinnaker to stall. The air flows into the spinnaker at a faster rate than it can exit. Eventually the sail fills with static air and, invariably, all drive is lost. This is one of the basic reasons why it nearly always pays to tack downwind, and never to run dead downward.

Fig. 62 shows the air flow when reaching. From this it will be seen that this spinnaker behaves exactly as a large jib, the air flowing across the sail from luff to leach. The spinnaker must be trimmed in the same manner as the jib on a reach. As with the jib, the spinnaker is at its most efficient setting when the luff is just about to lift.

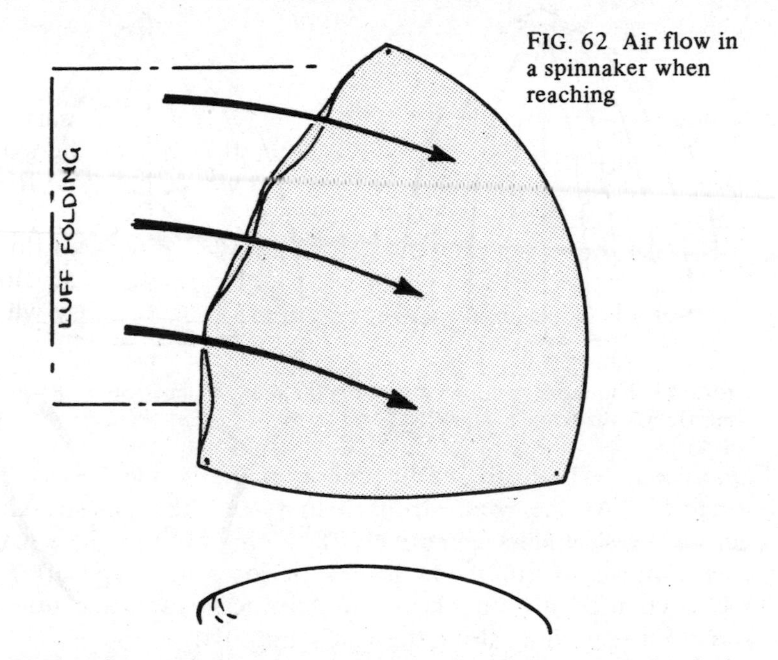

FIG. 62 Air flow in a spinnaker when reaching

Most class rules are quite strict in their control of the dimensions of the spinnaker but sailmakers can, by varying the cut of the spinnaker, produce a sail which will conform to the rule yet set differently from another. Most spinnaker materials stretch more across the bias than across the weft or warp. Therefore, by arranging the cut of the spinnaker, the stretch of the spinnaker in various directions can be controlled. Fig. 63 shows some of the more common cuts of

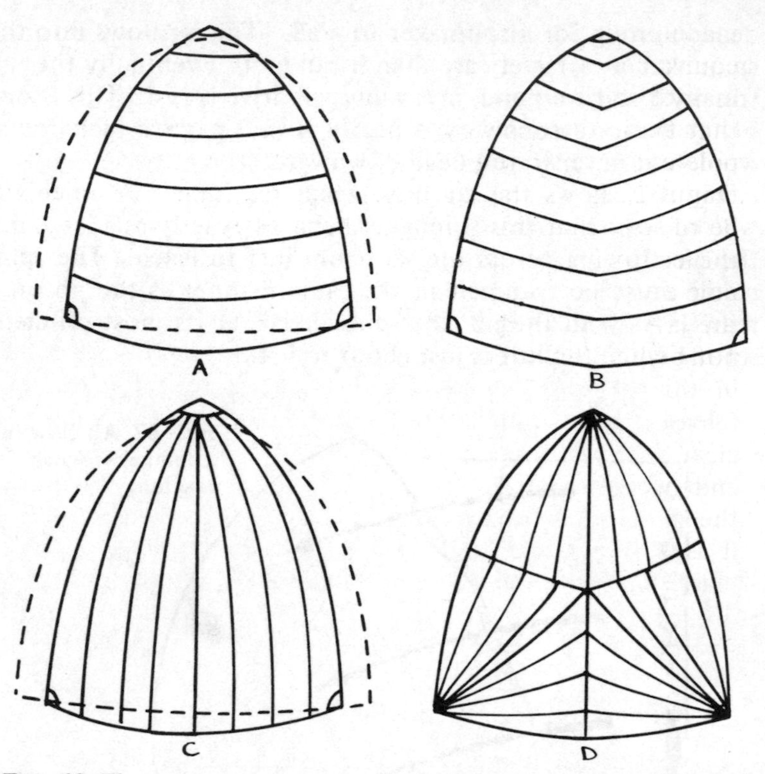

FIG. 63 The more common cuts of spinnaker: A–horizontal; B–isometric; C–vertical; D–star-cut

spinnaker. The horizontally cut spinnaker is ideal for small dinghies. As the wind strength increases, the sail stretches across the shoulders, effectively flattening the top. The main disadvantage of this type is that it loses its shape after it has been used a number of times in heavy weather, due to the cloth stretching along the leach and luff.

Equipment and Fittings

There are many different makes of equipment from which to choose when equipping a new boat. Choose the most suitable for easy spinnaker handling.

It is important to have a stiff spinnaker pole. Up to 5ft 6 in a pole can be made from one-inch-diameter aluminium alloy tube. Longer spinnaker poles, up to 8 ft 6 in, should be made from 1½-in diameter by 16 SWG aluminium tube or equivalent. The type of end-fittings should be one of the many piston-type ends available (Fig. 64). It is important that the eye on the mast is the correct size for the spinnaker pole end-fitting used. Matching eyes are available from most manufacturers of spinnaker pole ends. Centre fittings should be of the type shown. A trip line should be fitted, seized in the centre of the pole. The modern piston-type spinnaker pole-end, with a stainless-steel piston, should be used with the jaw opening upwards. The clew of the spinnaker should not be clipped directly to the spinnaker pole. Using the pole in this manner has two distinct advantages. Firstly, when releasing the spinnaker pole from the guy, the pole drops clear without any difficulty and, secondly, if the outboard end of the spinnaker pole should lift high in the air due to the uphaul/downhaul breaking or becoming disconnected, it is still possible to remove the spinnaker pole from the mast.

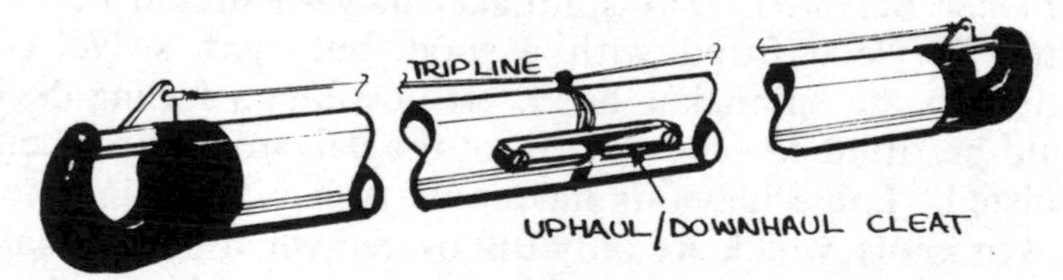

FIG. 64 Spinnaker pole with piston-type ends

Downhaul System. When the pole is in position, it is important that there should be no stretch in the uphaul/downhaul system. Many systems have shock cord in the positive part of the system which means that the height of the pole cannot always be controlled effectively. The only shock cord in the system illustrated (Fig. 65) is used to take the slack away, when the uphaul/downhaul is not in use. When in use, the load is taken by the eye on the mast, and the cleat in the boat. If two spinnaker pole eyes are used on the mast, spaced approximately one foot apart, and four knots are tied on the rope at four-inch intervals, the effective height of the outboard end of the spinnaker pole can be altered over a wide range.

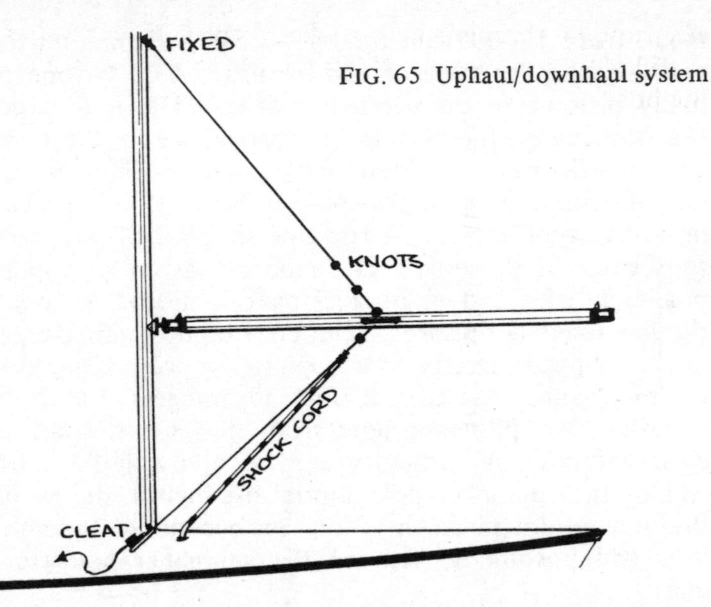

FIG. 65 Uphaul/downhaul system

Spinnaker Halyards. The spinnaker halyard should be hard-plaited Terylene fitted with a good, but light, swivel connection to the spinnaker head. If possible, a furling device should be fitted to take the tail of the halyard away, when it is hoisted. Loose halyards have a nasty habit of tying themselves in knots, which are only discovered when the spinnaker has to be lowered in a hurry. The halyard should be no larger than ½ in circumference, and should be led aft to a conveniently placed cleat for operation by the helmsman. This cleat should be a good quality cam cleat and it should be examined regularly for wear. There is nothing more embarrassing than a spinnaker slowly sinking towards the water, because the cleat has worn and will no longer hold.

Spinnaker Sheets. Soft-plaited 1-in circumference Terylene sheets should be used. When racing in light weather, a set of light sheets can be used, but the heavy sheets should always be carried, in case the wind increases in strength. The use of a continuous sheet not only reduces the total length of the rope required, but also means that there are two less rope ends in the boat to get tangled (Fig. 66). The length of the sheets should enable the pole to be set on the mast, with the guy running through the outboard end, whilst the spinnaker is still stored in its bag, with about 4 ft of sheet still slack in the boat.

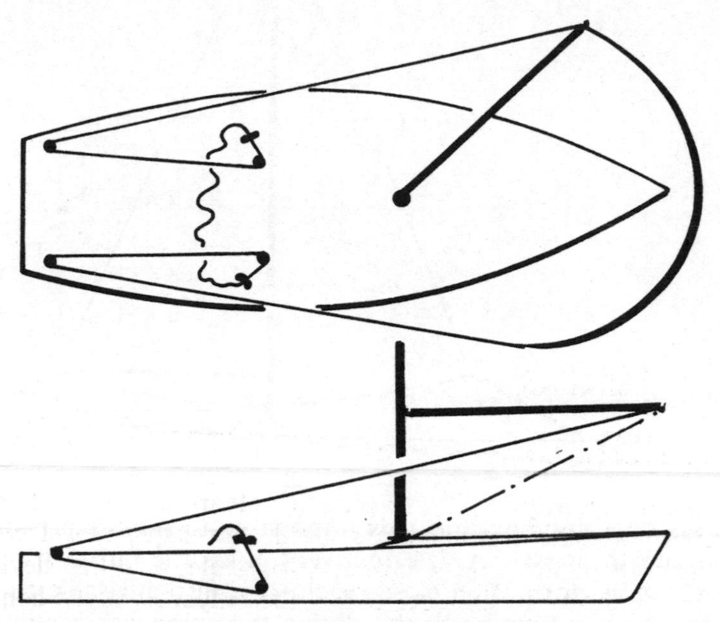

FIG. 66 Continuous spinnaker sheets

Deck Fittings. Fig. 67 shows a rough guide to the positioning of the sheet leads. They must also be placed so that they do not get in the way of the crew. Sheets should be led to a block opposite the crew, and a good cam cleat should be positioned above this block, in which the guy can be cleated. This cleat should be placed so that the crew, or the helmsman, can jam the guy. Care should be taken to reduce friction in the sheeting system, and it is recommended that large-diameter blocks are used. Where the sheet runs across the deck for some distance, a small bulls-eye should be fitted, lifting the sheet clear of the deck. This will considerably reduce the friction, especially when the sheets are wet.

A reaching hook should be fitted. The usual position for this hook is just in front of the shrouds, the actual position depending on the shape of the boat. This fitting is essential

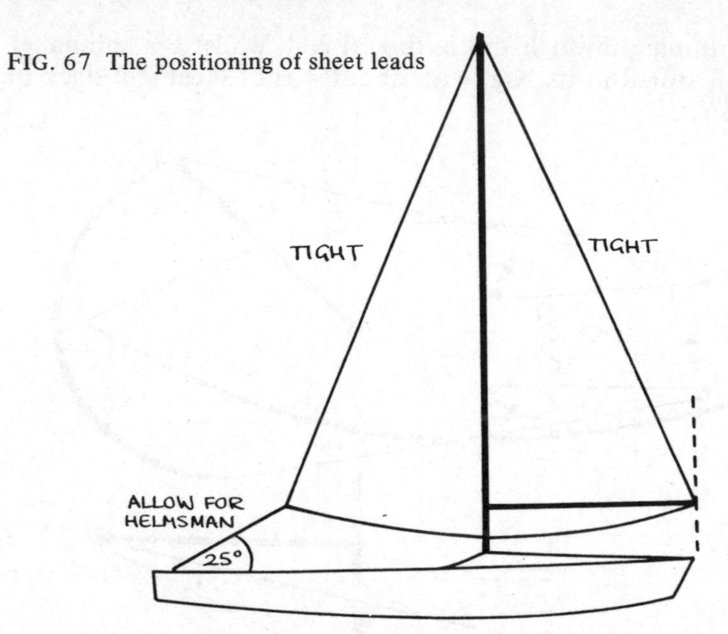

FIG. 67 The positioning of sheet leads

on all trapezing boats, as it is impossible to trapeze properly underneath a guy. As it effectively holds the outboard end of the pole down on a close reach, it is also advisable to fit these to non-trapezing boats. When the spinnaker is stowed the halyard can be led through these hooks, keeping it clear of the jib. This should be taken into account, when deciding the final position of these fittings.

Spinnaker Stowage. Provision should be made to stow the spinnaker on either side of the mast. The spinnaker should be stowed clear of the floor of the boat, and kept as dry as possible.

Cleats should be fitted for the stowage of the sheets and halyards.

Spinnaker Chutes. The spinnaker chute is, perhaps, the most significant development in the dinghy classes since the introduction of Terylene sails and metal masts. This device, invented by Americans for use in the Flying Dutchman class, has been adopted by a number of dinghy classes. Fig. 68 shows the principle of the chute.

FIG. 68 The spinnaker chute

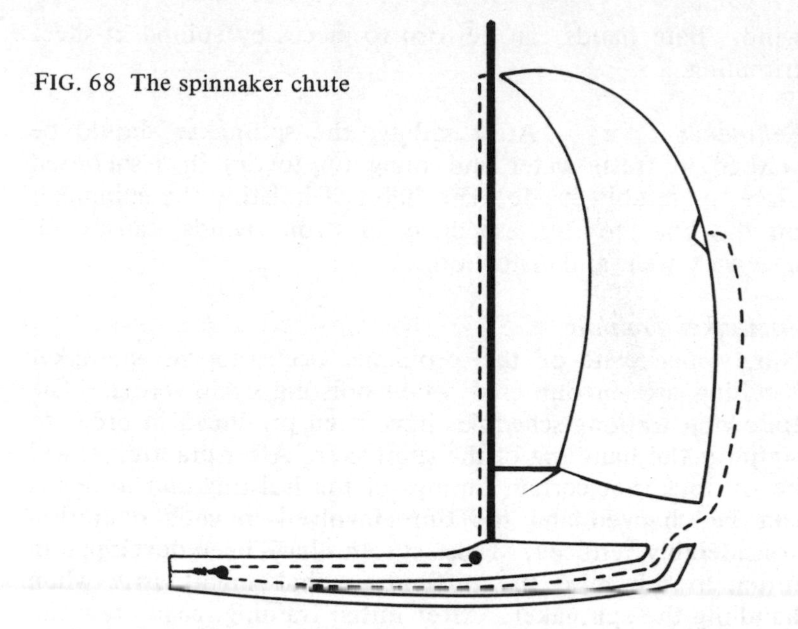

The training schedules in this chapter are designed for boats with normal spinnaker stowage, but they can quite easily be adapted for use in training on boats fitted with a spinnaker chute.

Jib Furling. The facility of being able to furl the jib is definitely an advantage, when learning to use the spinnaker. Initial training should be carried out with the jib furled, enabling the crew to concentrate on the spinnaker. When using the spinnaker in very light airs, it often pays to furl the jib, especially in boats, such as the Flying Dutchman class, which have a large overlapping Genoa.

Gloves. Playing the spinnaker sheet entails the recovery and release of many feet of rope quite rapidly, and the crew often has a number of turns of the spinnaker sheet wrapped round the hands. Although, at one time, the appearance of a crew wearing gloves was a sure cue for sarcasm from the opposition, most top crews now feel that they are an essential item of clothing to be worn when racing. The comfort of gloves is appreciated most when spinnaker reaching in heavy wind. Bare hands can be torn to pieces by spinnaker-sheet trimming.

Spinnaker Care. After sailing, the spinnaker should be washed in fresh water and hung up to dry in a sheltered place, preferably inside. The habit of hoisting the spinnaker on the boat to dry, especially in strong winds, causes unnecessary wear and distortion.

Spinnaker Training
Ninety per cent of the problems occurring in spinnaker handling are encountered when hoisting or lowering. The following training schedules have been produced in order to simplify the handling of the spinnaker. After practice, it will be obvious that certain timings of the hoisting and lowering can be changed and the time involved in each operation considerably reduced. These systems have been developed in order to minimise the difficulties that might arise when handling the spinnaker. After initial training, each crew can develop their own version of these systems to suit their boat and their method of sailing. In the first stages of spinnaker training, the actual setting of the spinnaker should not be considered too critically. Once the crews have learned to hoist and lower the spinnaker with confidence, they can then concentrate on the finer points of spinnaker setting.

Leeward Spinnaker Hoist (Figs. 69a–f)

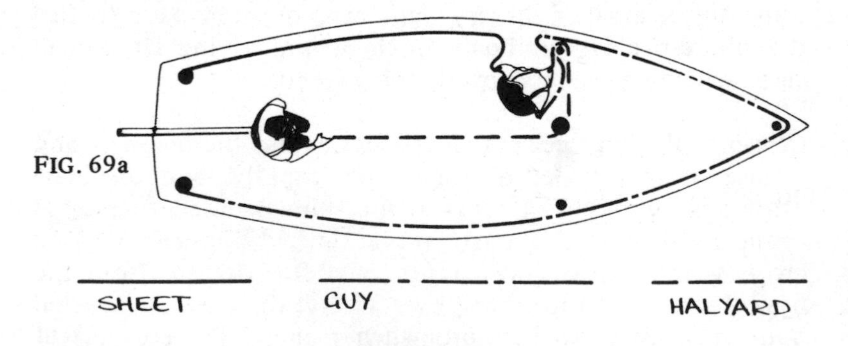

FIG. 69a

Spinnaker stowed to leeward, halyard led aft to helmsman.

FIG. 69b

Stage 1
Helmsman: Prepare to pass spinnaker pole to crew.
Crew: Free spinnaker sheets and halyard. Clear spinnaker for hoisting.

FIG. 69c

Stage 2
Helmsman: Pass pole to crew and balance boat.

FIG. 69d

Stage 3
Crew: Clip pole to guy, fit up haul/downhaul and clip pole to mast.

FIG. 69e

Stage 4
Helmsman: Hoist and cleat spinnaker; free sheet.
Crew: Adjust and cleat guy.

Stage 5
Helmsman: Adjust sheet if crew is still adjusting guy.
Crew: Adjust and play sheet.

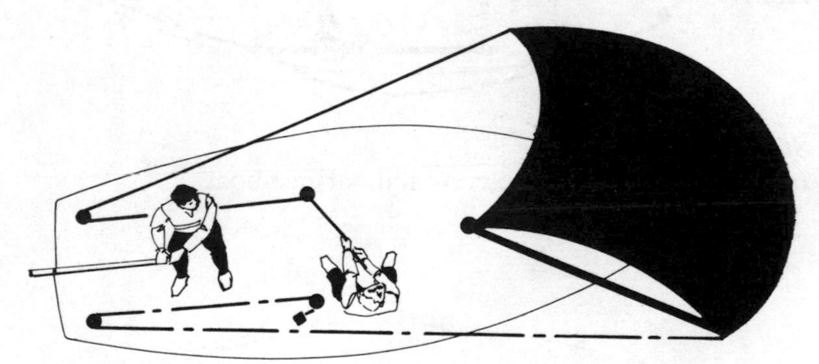

FIG. 69f

Stage 6
Helmsman: If necessary sit to leeward so crew can sit to windward.
Crew: Sit to windward. Must have clear view of spinnaker luff and wind indicators.
After practice, helmsman can carry out his part of Stage 4 whilst crew carries out his part of Stage 3.

Windward Spinnaker Hoist (Figs. 70a–g)

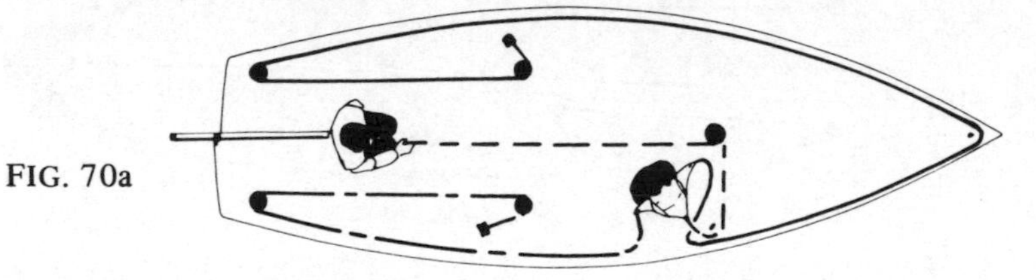

FIG. 70a

Spinnaker stowed to windward, halyard led aft to helmsman.

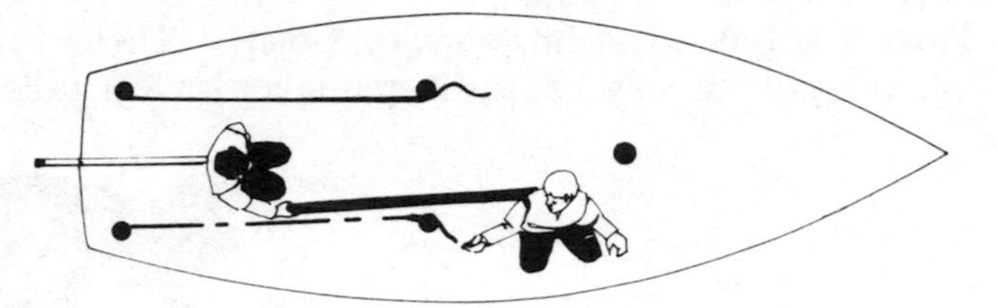

FIG. 70b

Stage 1
Helmsman: Prepare to pass pole to crew.
Crew: Free sheets, guy and halyard if necessary.

FIG. 70c

Stage 2
Helmsman: Place pole in position for crew to pick up easily.
Crew: Check guy, set and cleat so that windward clew can reach forestay.

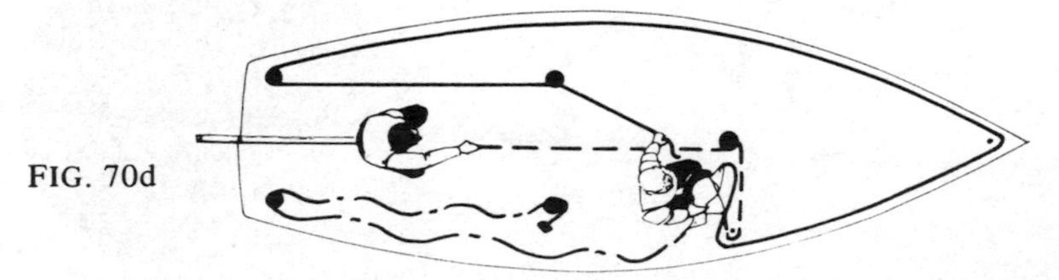

FIG. 70d

Stage 3
Helmsman: Take up slack in spinnaker halyard.
Crew: Pick up spinnaker in as tight a bundle as possible, hold sheet in other hand.

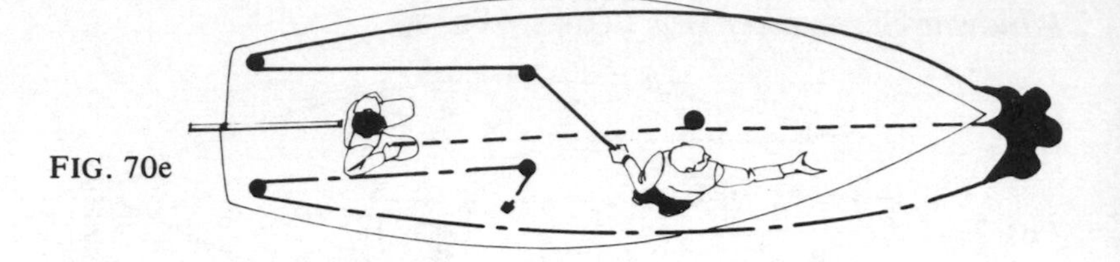

FIG. 70e

Stage 4
Helmsman: Steer downwind and hoist when crew hails. Bear away on to run if necessary.
Crew: Shout to helmsman to hoist. Throw spinnaker forward, pulling on sheet until spinnaker is clear to leeward.

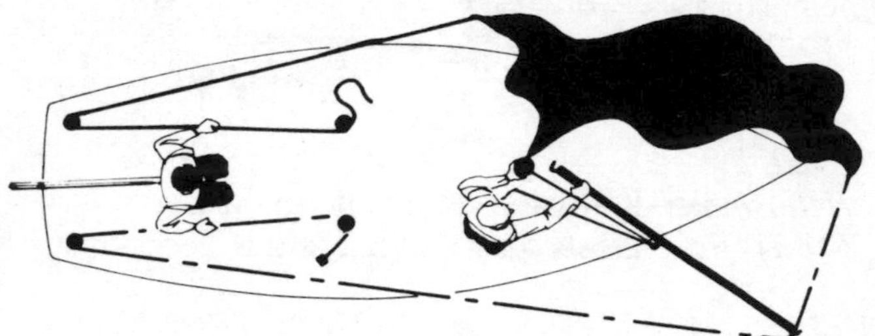

FIG. 70f

Stage 5
Helmsman: Come back on course.
Crew: Fit pole, adjust, and cleat guy.

Stage 6
Helmsman: Set spinnaker sheet.
Crew: Take sheet from helmsman.

FIG. 70g

Stage 7
Helmsman: If necessary sit to leeward so crew can sit to windward.
Crew: Sit to windward. Re-cleat guy. Must have clear view of spinnaker luff and wind indicators.

Lowering Spinnaker (Figs 71a–d)

FIG. 71a

Stage 1
Crew: Ease guy forward. Remove spinnaker pole and pass to helmsman.

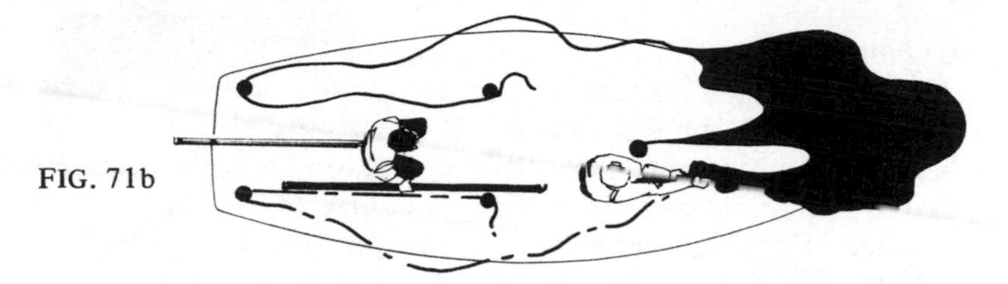

FIG. 71b

Stage 2
Helmsman: Take and stow spinnaker pole.
Crew: Release sheet.

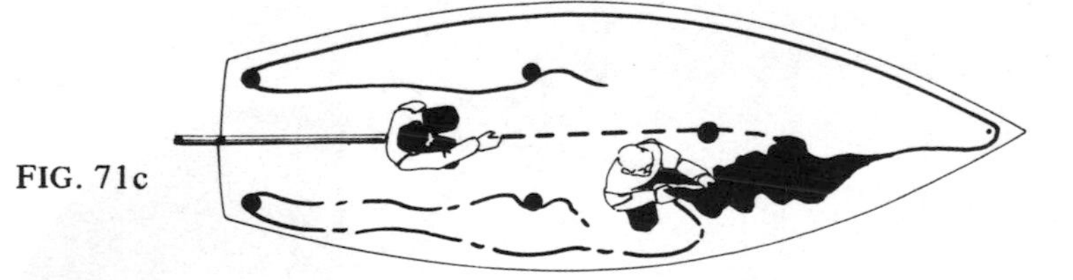

FIG. 71c

Stage 3
Crew: Standing by the windward side of the mast, take the guy and gather in the foot of the spinnaker until the leeward clew passes round the forestay.

Stage 4
Helmsman: Release halyard on crew's instructions.
Crew: Indicate to helmsman to release halyard. Stow spinnaker by working down windward luff. Finally gather, and stow, rest of foot.

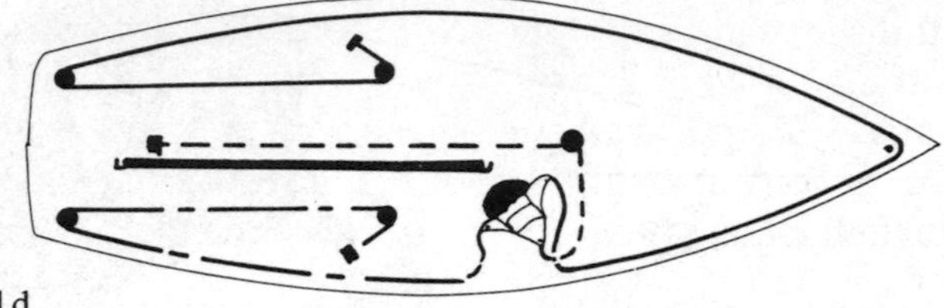

FIG. 71d

Stage 5

Crew: Tidy, and cleat, halyards and sheets.
Helmsman can often tidy sheets whilst crew is stowing spinnaker. This depends on boat layout.

Gybing

The execution of a good gybe is, almost entirely, the responsibility of the helmsman. If the course steered by the helmsman is correct, the actual gybing of the sails becomes easy. Fig. 72 shows the optimum course to be taken when gybing. Obviously it is not always possible to follow this course due to the proximity of other boats and various obstructions. The boat which turns sharply from one gybe to the other not only loses speed when turning, but invariably ends up with the spinnaker collapsed.

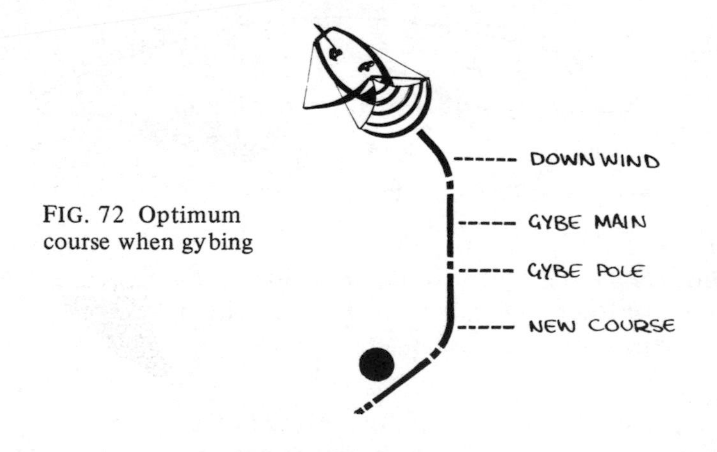

FIG. 72 Optimum course when gybing

When the boat reaches the point of gybing with the wind almost dead astern, the crew should centre the spinnaker and cleat the sheet and guy. Marks on the sheets and guy, showing when the spinnaker is exactly central, will be found to be a great aid. The mainsail should then be gybed slowly. In the case of a centre mainsheet, the gybe should be controlled by the helmsman holding the falls of the mainsheet: in the case of an aft mainsheet, by the crew using the kicking strap. The mainsail should be allowed to gybe as slowly as possible. If the mainsail slams across, it will cause the spinnaker to collapse. The jib should be gybed at the same time as the mainsail.

The pole is released from the mast clip and clipped onto the new guy. The old guy is released from the other end of the pole, using the trip line, and the spinnaker pole clipped onto the mast. The downhaul fittings, described previously, should not release themselves during this operation; it should not therefore be necessary to adjust the uphaul/downhaul when carrying out this operation. The helmsman should assist the crew by trimming the spinnaker sheets during the spinnaker pole changeover. The crew then takes the sheet from the helmsman, checks the guy setting, and the gybe is complete.

Gybing the Spinnaker (Figs 73a–d)

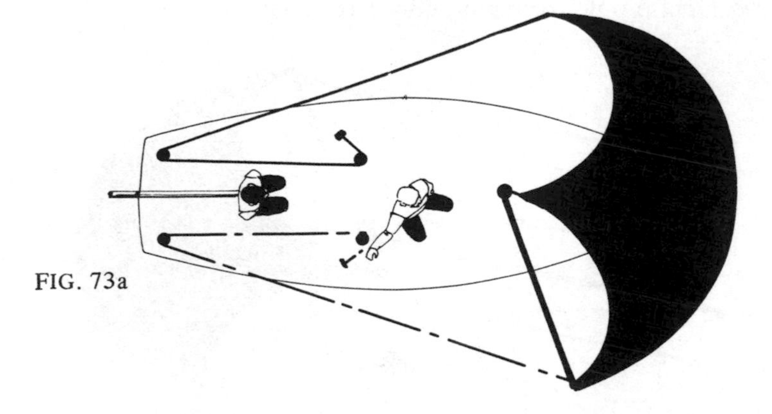

FIG. 73a

Stage 1
Helmsman: Square off on to dead run.
Crew: Centre spinnaker and cleat sheet and guy.

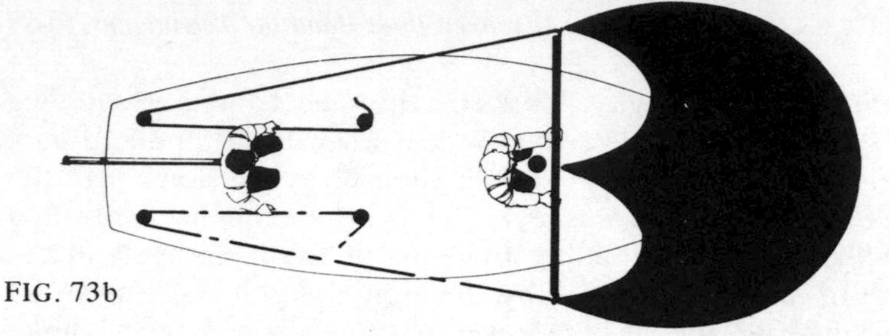

FIG. 73b

Stage 2
Helmsman: Gybe mainsail slowly, pausing amidships.
Crew: Gybe jib. Unclip pole from mast, clip to sheet.

FIG. 73c

Stage 3
Helmsman: Play new sheet to keep spinnaker full.
Crew: Unclip pole from guy, clip it to mast.

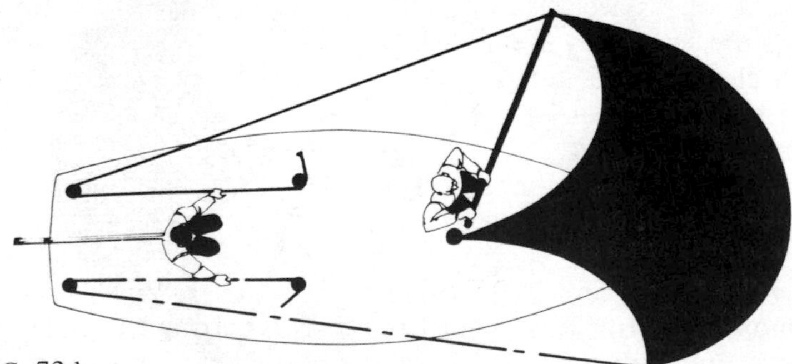

FIG. 73d

Stage 4
Helmsman: Luff up on to new course.
Crew: Trim guy and sheet as required.

Spinnaker Setting
The spinnaker pole should be set at approximately 90° to the apparent wind direction. When the wind is ahead of the beam, the pole should be held just off the forestay. Sheets should be adjusted so that the luff of the spinnaker is just about to collapse. The sheet should be played continuously, remembering that it is very easy to over-sheet the spinnaker. This problem can be very easily avoided. The crew should always be easing the sheet out until the spinnaker is about to collapse. If the spinnaker starts to fold, the sheet should be recovered rapidly, and then slowly eased out again once the spinnaker is set. When a gust hits the boat, the sheet should be eased and the helmsman should bear away. If this is timed correctly, the boat will increase speed considerably. A number of books recommend that the guy should be brought aft at the same time, but the loads of modern high-performance boats make it almost impossible. It is better to concentrate on playing the spinnaker sheet and keeping the boat upright than to try to play the guy. In very light weather it is possible to trim the sheet and guy at the same time, but, as soon as the wind increases above force 2, the guy should be cleated and the crew should concentrate fully on keeping the spinnaker sheet trimmed correctly.

Pole Height
Most books state that the pole height is correct when the clews are level. In practice it is often rather difficult to see both clews at the same time. It is therefore better to set the pole so that, when the luff lifts, it does so over the maximum possible length. This means that the spinnaker is setting correctly over the maximum possible area. Surprisingly it will then be found that the clews are level.

Steering During Spinnaker Hoisting
In most modern boats, whilst the crew is setting the pole and sheets, the helmsman must hoist the spinnaker. This normally requires both hands and it is therefore necessary to devise some other method of steering. The usual technique is to steer the boat with the tiller between the legs. This, of course, needs to be practised before attempting to hoist the

spinnaker for the first time. If it is necessary to hold the tiller in the hand, do not take hold of the tiller between the legs, but hold the extension behind the back with the hand on the leeward side of the boat (Fig. 74). If the helmsman has to move rapidly to the windward side, in order to trim the boat, it is very easy to move from this position.

FIG. 74 Helmsman using tiller extension during spinnaker hoisting

Shore Drill

1. Note how spinnaker pole is stowed in boat.
2. Place pole in position on mast and check setting of uphaul/downhaul.
3. Examine the position of cleats for guy and spinnaker stowage.
4. Stow spinnaker and fasten sheets and halyard.
5. If wind is very light, or the boat can be placed in a sheltered spot, the spinnaker should be hoisted, set and stowed.

Afloat Drill

1. Practise steering with tiller between legs whilst standing.
2. Fit pole and stow pole ten times.
3. Hoist and set spinnaker from leeward position, then stow when 30 yards sailed. Hoist and set spinnaker, then stow when 30 yards sailed. Gybe. Then repeat five times.
4. Hoist and set spinnaker, run 200 yards (jib furled), gybe, repeat ten times.
5. Repeat 4 with jib set.

6. Practise reaching with jib furled.
7. Reach with jib set.
8. Reach with crew on trapeze.

Conclusion

Practice is the only way to learn how to use a spinnaker correctly. Each spinnaker requires to be set differently in order to give maximum performance. For example, when reaching with a horizontally cut spinnaker, the pole has to be set high, but, when reaching with a star-cut spinnaker, the pole has to be set very low. It is fairly easy to learn how to hoist and lower a spinnaker, but the actual trimming of a spinnaker can only be learned by practice. This point cannot be emphasised too strongly.

Index